FROM PANIC TO POWER

FROM PANIC *to* POWER

❧ *Proven Techniques to Calm Your Anxieties, Conquer Your Fears, and Put You in Control of Your Life*

LUCINDA BASSETT

■ HarperCollins*Publishers*

Designed by Irving Perkins Associates

Library of Congress Cataloging-in-Publication Data

Bassett, Lucinda.
    From panic to power : proven techniques to calm your anxieties, conquer your fears, and put you in control of your life/Lucinda Bassett.—1st ed.
      p. cm.
    ISBN 0-06-017320-3
    1. Anxiety. 2. Fear. 3. Stress (Psychology) 4. Stress management.
5. Panic attacks. 6. Adjustment (Psychology)
I. Title.
BF575.A6B34   1995
152.4'6—dc20   95-21052

---

95 96 97 98 99 ❖/HC 10 9 8 7 6 5

This book is dedicated to my sister, Donna.
"Sisters, sisters, there were never such devoted sisters..."
I miss you.

CONTENTS

ACKNOWLEDGMENTS

Thanks to my husband, David, for being my best friend for thirteen years, for believing in me, for loving me so intensely and unconditionally, and for helping me to shine. Your hard work and dedication to the cause has played a major role in the growth and success of the Midwest Center. Here's to the future.

Thanks to my children, Brittany and Sammy, for putting up with me at my desk, night after night, day after day, while I was writing, writing, writing. Brittany, I really loved it when you snuck in to sit with me. Thanks for all the back rubs! Sammy, your funny little songs and dances kept me going. "I'm so...lucky." Having you two has been the greatest accomplishment of my life.

Thanks to Carolyn Dickman, my dear, dear friend and colleague. God blessed me when he sent you to the Midwest Center. Thank you for being a friend and confidant. What would I do without you? What would the Midwest Center do without you? What would we all do without you? What a gift you are!

Thanks to Dr. Phil Fisher. You have been there since the beginning, offering insight and support, but most of all, unwavering faith in me and my mission. You are a very special man and I will always be grateful for your friendship.

A big thanks to Margret McBride—wow! What a

woman! You are the reason this book came to be. The absolute best literary agent I could ask for. What a total pleasure it is knowing you and working with you. Thank you for encouraging me to keep this book "from the heart."

Thanks to Diane Reverand for being a fabulous editor and friend. Thank you for believing in the message from the moment we met. Your energy, enthusiasm, and insight as an editor were wonderful. Thanks for supporting and encouraging the positive message in this book. And a big thanks to HarperCollins Publishers for all their marketing efforts.

A very special thanks to Andrea Cagan. I believe you truly were meant to work with me on this book. I can't imagine a smoother, more enjoyable collaboration. You are a very warm, special, talented woman. Working with you was a very natural "predestined" experience. Thank you for helping me make this book the best it could be.

Thanks to Barb Banky for treating the Midwest Center as if it were your home away from home. You have given so much of yourself to help me help others. I love you for it.

Thanks to Dr. Jim Buldas, Dr. Paul Kelley, Tracy Thorbahn, Monica Dickman, Diana Romstadt, Jacque Maki, Dr. Joel Swabb, Mike Glugosh, Connie Szollosi, Lisa Reiter, Jo Hudson for all your hard work and dedication through the years. You have made it possible for us to spread "our" wings. What a special group of people you are.

Thanks to my brother Michael for using your tremendous talents and creative energy to get the message out worldwide. Your music and television production skills have taken us to a whole new level. I love you.

Thanks to Tim Redel for a wonderful experience in shooting the cover for this book. You had me climbing ominous mountains and soaring with the birds by the seashore. What wonderful memories. Let's do it again sometime.

Thanks to all the professionals who use our techniques to help their clients help themselves. With the combination of your support and these skills, people can't help but recover from anxiety.

Finally thanks to all the people around the world who have believed in me enough to use these techniques to help themselves. Your letters, phone calls, and personal stories of struggle and triumph have been a tremendous source of inspiration. You are why I do what I do.

INTRODUCTION

Everyone wants to feel confident. We all want to know that we are capable of greatness, that we are strong, powerful, and very creative. We want to be in control of our lives and to succeed in making our dreams come true. The truth is, we are and we can. Greatness is our birthright.

Just as greatness is a natural part of who we are, anxiety and fear are also a part of everyone's lives. When we feel we are in control, we can keep our lives balanced and most everything runs smoothly. When we allow anxiety and fear to dominate, we start questioning our every move. The mere anticipation of these dreaded emotions can turn a potentially pleasant situation into a misery and a nightmare. When anxiety rules, your physical and emotional energy are drained to the point that everything is colored by worry and discomfort. Then your life becomes an endurance test rather than a celebration.

I lived a great deal of my life controlled by a serious anxiety disorder. It may sound strange, but now I consider my anxiety a gift. Yes, that's right. A gift. After suffering for years with fear and dread, along with a host of debilitating physical symptoms, I was finally forced to do something about it. Once my feelings of "being out of control" had escalated to where I felt that I could no longer function, I started to look for answers.

In my search for help, hope, and a better life, I found

something wonderful. Something that I didn't know was missing. Something that I didn't know I needed. I found security. I found that I am my own security. I didn't find it "out there." Instead, I found a powerful untapped source of strength and healing right here inside myself. This wonderful sense of inner security has gotten me through many a difficult challenge. Now I understand without exception that I am my own safe person and my own safe place. No matter what difficulties life brings, I can take care of me.

As a result of my struggles with anxiety and agoraphobia—which I define as fear of fearful feelings and thoughts often leading to avoidance behaviors—I have been blessed with my ability to help others who are suffering as I did. In 1983, along with a dear friend and gifted doctor, Phil Fisher, M.D., I founded the Midwest Center for Stress and Anxiety, Inc. During the past twelve years, we have been fortunate in assembling a staff of such highly dedicated people as Carolyn Dickman, our Education Director, and Barb Banky, Director of Operations. Together, we have helped tens of thousands of people find their security. Some of them suffer panic attacks, anxiety gone so far out of control that breathing becomes difficult, equilibrium flies out the window, stomachs seize up, and minds feel bewildered and confused. Some of our clients have spent most of their lives avoiding people and things due to their agoraphobia. Others have experienced obsessive, scary thoughts. Still others had exhausted themselves with their compulsive behaviors.

By the time I met them, many of these people had spent small fortunes looking for help. They hadn't found it. Some of them were on medications that didn't work or only worked for a little while; others couldn't tolerate medication or were afraid of it. There were many who didn't have severe anxiety, but they felt nervous, stressed out, and uncomfortable far too often. They overreacted and worried excessively. Ultimately, anxiety controlled their lives and kept them from being truly happy.

You might be wondering if this book is for you. Am I anxious enough to need this book? Am I too anxious for it to work? The answer is, anxiety has no prejudices; it attacks everyone. It's a thief. It robs us of our present happiness by filling us with anticipatory worry. It makes us feel insecure and question our abilities. It makes us physically sick. If anxiety is disrupting your life to any degree, this book can help you.

Whether we are suffering from severe anxiety or a less intense but underlying sense of discomfort and stress, we all have something in common. We want to feel better. We want to stop the vicious cycle of anxiety, fear, and worry. We want to feel relaxed, secure, in control, and at peace. We want to enjoy each day, to feel excited about our lives, to be willing and able to take risks, to do whatever we want to do without debilitating fear or anticipation. Is that really possible? Absolutely.

I suffered with anxiety and phobias all of my life. As a child, I had scary thoughts and bad dreams. My father's alcoholism created chaos and additional feelings of insecurity. As a teenager, I suffered from eating disorders and irritable bowel syndrome. I began avoiding situations where I couldn't come and go as I pleased, situations where I couldn't be in control.

By age nineteen, I was having panic attacks regularly. College was a real challenge because it was difficult for me to sit in class. I felt anxious, panicky, and trapped. I made all kinds of excuses for my lack of social activity and my inability to travel with friends. Riding in the back seat of cars and flying on planes was extremely difficult. My world became smaller and smaller.

By my early twenties, I was a top producer selling advertising for a major radio station in Toledo, Ohio. In spite of my anxiety, I was doing well, but no one knew how I suffered. No one knew why I didn't ride in the car with my sales manager on sales calls, or why I couldn't sit in meetings for hours with the doors closed. No one knew that I started every day with anticipation, fear, and dread. I was able to keep up a front because, as badly as I felt most of the time, this job gave me the freedom to come and go as I pleased. I wasn't physically confined or controlled. I knew that as long as I performed, I'd be okay.

I wasn't okay. As time passed, my anxiety got worse. I began to see doctors and psychiatrists. No one had any answers. Finally, one morning, after a long, difficult night of anxiety and panic, my prayer was answered. I saw a woman on a talk show describing anxiety and its symptoms. She was talking about something called agoraphobia. I listened. There was a name for it! She was talking about me! I wasn't alone!

I went to the library and read everything I could find about anxiety, agoraphobia, and panic disorder. I spent the next six months educating myself and searching for answers. I began to see that I was causing much of my anxiety by the way that I thought. I was creating most of my body symptoms by the way my mind chose to react to things. I started thinking and reacting differently. By taking control of my fears, I began to feel better. I began doing things I had been avoiding like flying, driving distances, and socializing.

Coincidentally, at the time that I was making all of these changes, I also changed insurance companies and consequently I had to find a new physician. I heard about a man named Dr. Philip Fisher, who was reputed to be a wonderful doctor. I scheduled an appointment. I feel very strongly that it was fate; we hit it off right away. In the course of our conversation, I mentioned that I had suffered from anxiety and panic attacks. So impressed by my story and my self-recovery, he asked if I would be interested in doing groups with him for people with anxiety-related problems. I agreed.

That was thirteen years ago. That's how it all began. The news spread by word of mouth that people were being helped, that people who had suffered for years were recovering. Many of them were getting off their anti-anxiety medications. Doctors and psychiatrists were referring clients; they came from other states, driving as much as five hours one way to participate in our outpatient groups. I often spent my nights at home, talking people through panic attacks into the wee hours of the morning. What a great feeling it was to help someone else feel better! To help someone get through the moment. To help someone get through the night. To be able to give someone else hope.

When something works, word travels fast. In a very short period of time, we were receiving calls from all over the country. People wanted help. That's when I created the Attacking Anxiety audio cassette self-help program. With the encouragement and guidance of both Phil Fisher and my husband David, I sat at my computer and wrote. I spent most of my spare time researching in the library, although much of what I've learned came from the years of groups I cofacilitated with Dr. Fisher. After a full year of writing, researching, and taping, the audio program was finished and ready to be distributed.

When you are on a mission and are absolutely committed, I believe that providence moves in miraculous ways. All kinds of things happen that you don't expect and never would have dreamed possible. My Attacking Anxiety program took off in a way that still amazes me. Today, it is being used in clinics, hospitals, and schools across the country. Thousands have benefited from it and many of these people eventually have been able to stop their medications. Therapists around the world use my program as the backbone of their treatment program for anxiety disorders.

I went on to join professional organizations such as the Anxiety Disorders Association of America and the National Speakers Association. My techniques became well known and I was asked to speak at various conferences. At the suggestion of a highly respected Toledo businessman who went through my program, I offered a stress management program to a Toledo-based company. It consisted of the same skills offered in my Attacking Anxiety program. That was the starting point of many years of my work with major corporations, such as AT&T, McDonald's, Chrysler Corporation, Ford Motor Corporation, Merck Pharmaceuticals, the Medical College of Ohio, and St. Vincent Medical Center. I'm proud to say that many of my corporate clients feel that this program is one of the best they have ever offered to their employees. Everybody has anxiety, even if they call it something else.

Can you really turn panic into power? The answer is unequivocally YES! I've done it. And not only have I conquered my fear; I've had a great time in the process. I've talked about anxiety and shared my knowledge on national talk shows with Oprah Winfrey, Regis and Kathy Lee, Maury Povich, and many others. One of my most exciting achievements was when I was asked to tell my story in the Great Comebacks issue of *Success* magazine.

If you feel anxious, fearful, overwhelmed, or stressed out too often, I've been where you are. Now, I am completely recovered. Once I put an end to all the negativity, fear, and worry my anxiety created, I was able to use my time and energy in a positive way to accomplish things even beyond my dreams. Today, my life's mission is to help you do the same for yourself.

This book is about transformation, about conquering

your anxiety, panic, and fear, and turning them into personal power, success, and peace of mind. These skills will help you to acquire a whole new sense of confidence, self-worth, strength, and real security that won't go away. You will gain the insight, guidance, and motivation to go from panic to power, to live the life you have always dreamed of. If I can do it, so can you.

❦ *Whatever you can do, or dream you can, begin it.*
  Boldness has genius, power and magic in it.

  —GOETHE

  Lucinda Bassett
  May 1995

PART 1

DISCOVERY

CHAPTER 1

ALL THINGS ARE POSSIBLE

✣ *Come to the edge, He said.*
They said, We are afraid.
Come to the edge, He said.
They came.
He pushed them...
And they flew.

—GUILLAUME APOLLINAIRE

Here's the good news: you're special. If you are someone who experiences more than the average amount of anxiety, you are full of potential for greatness. Why? Because you probably have above average intelligence. You are highly creative with a fabulous imagination. You are detail-oriented and analytical. These are wonderful traits that can make you extremely successful and enable you to accomplish great things. Unfortunately, people with anxiety disorders tend to use their attributes to scare themselves. They overintellectualize, overanalyze, and use their creativity to envision the worst possible scenarios. Used in a negative way, our wonderful traits can make us sick.

Let's pretend for a moment that you could turn all this

anxious energy around and make it work *for* you instead of *against* you. Can you imagine how different your life might be? Ask yourself where you might be right now if anxiety and fear weren't holding you back. If anything were possible. What would you do differently if you weren't afraid to fail or to succeed, if you weren't afraid of anxious feelings or being alone? What if you weren't afraid to take chances, to get involved, or even to embarrass yourself a little? Your whole life might be different. You might be living somewhere else or working somewhere else. Possibly you would have different relationships. Or maybe you would be right where you are, but you'd be enjoying it a whole lot more. It's not too late.

✡ **You are on the verge of change.**

A CALL TO FREEDOM

With this book, you can go to the edge and free yourself from anxiety. You can find freedom and take charge of your life, now and forever. As wonderful as that sounds, I know it also sounds scary. You need to trust yourself and know that you have all the tools necessary to get on the road to recovery and to build a good life for yourself. You just need a good foundation.

When you embark on a learning process that will most assuredly change your life forever, don't you want to learn from someone who has overcome those debilitating fears? When you learn from someone who has done it, you can be reassured and motivated. That's where I come in. I've been there and I've made it out the other side.

For many, many years I made excuses for why my life wasn't going the way I wanted it to. My anxiety was a frightening experience, but at the same time it was also my protection. My constant fears and body symptoms—feelings of bewilderment, heart palpitations, dizziness—gave me reasons not to do the things that really scared me, like taking chances, ending unhealthy relationships, standing up for and depending upon myself. I spent many years of my life feeling different from other people. I had scary thoughts about losing control. I often worried that I would embarrass myself or the people close to me.

I had always considered myself independent. Energetic as a child, creative and fun loving as a teenager, I loved to have fun and do exciting things. Yet, I remember having scary thoughts as young as seven years old. By the age of nine, I had developed an eating disorder. The sight of food made me sick. Secretly, I thought I was dying of some horrible disease. Despite a substantial weight loss, I appeared happy, but I wasn't.

As time passed, the eating problems dissipated and I developed another anxiety-related problem: irritable bowel syndrome. This frustrating problem is common to many people with anxiety disorder. By fourteen, everything in my life revolved around my fear of diarrhea. I made excuses about my comings and goings. My activities were extremely limited. I couldn't enjoy my teenage years.

What happened to me is what happens to so many people. One fear created another. By my sixteenth birthday, a time when I should have been focused on boys and school, I was in a constant state of worry. I remember watching the news and hearing the usual stories about someone jumping out a window or hurting someone else and I would think, "What if I did that?" Of course I didn't tell anyone about my thoughts. There might have been something wrong with me and I didn't want anyone else to think I was strange. By the time I was eighteen, I was experiencing panic attacks regularly, feeling uncomfortable in any situation where I couldn't run if need be. I began making excuses for myself. The simplest things were difficult for me.

One of my most difficult challenges was being in an unhealthy relationship. I knew I should leave, but I was so insecure about being alone, I couldn't end it. It turned out that I didn't have to; he ended it. Once on my own, I moved a few times and changed jobs and, although I was full of fear, anxiety, and self-doubt, I functioned. I somehow managed to stay in my comfort zone, physically and emotionally.

By my early twenties, I wondered if I was losing my mind. Insanity was my biggest fear back then. I remember driving miles out of my way to avoid passing a state psychiatric hospital, so afraid I might end up there. The interesting thing is that most people didn't notice my strange behavior. Even those closest to me didn't know about my hidden fears. This is typical.

❧**When we are in an anxious episode, we think the whole world notices the things we do, yet very few people really do.**

Everyone is focused on his own life just as we are.

Feeling Out of Control

I was working hard during this period and by many standards was quite a successful woman. Outward appearances suggested that I was confident, independent, secure, and career-focused. Inside, I was full of turmoil. I worried from morning until night about my body. Would I make it through the day? Would I lose control in a meeting and have to leave? Could others sense my discomfort? My family knew I was having problems but they didn't understand what they were and they didn't know what to do for me. They had no frame of reference for my fears and scary thoughts.

It was around this time that I met my husband David. He was fun, outgoing, and interesting, but what was most appealing to me was his lack of inhibition. He didn't worry. He didn't overreact. I was the type of person who would obsess for weeks or even months about what someone said about me. David's favorite line was, "Hey, you want to talk about me, get in line." He really didn't care.

Sometimes he frustrated me because he was so carefree. Nothing "got to him." Everything got to me. I would get mad at him for what I called his insensitivity. At the same time, I envied it. Why couldn't I be more like him? Since our personalities were so different, he found it difficult to understand my anxiety. I couldn't help him out. How could I explain my panic attacks to him when I couldn't even understand them myself?

I remember once when David and two friends stopped by in a little VW bug. It was a spontaneous visit; they were on their way to an art festival in Ann Arbor, Michigan, which was two hours away. David wanted me to go along. Taking one look at the tiny back seat of that car, I instantly became upset and anxious. I didn't know why, but I absolutely could not crawl in there and ride for two hours. I didn't go. I felt bad inside. "What's happened to me?" I thought. "I used to be so independent. I used to go places and do things." My boundaries were getting smaller.

In spite of my anxiety, David made our relationship romantic. He was a romantic man and his idea of adventure meant travel. One time, he booked a trip for us to Mexico. I was terrified about the flight, about staying in another country, and about vacationing far from home. I worked myself into a panic before we even left with all my "what-if" thinking. What if I lost my mind over there and no one could understand me? What if I lost control in the airplane? What if they put me in a hospital there and I couldn't get out? Needless to say, it was not a pleasant trip for me. I ruined the experience with constant worry. Each tourist attraction was a dreaded event. I didn't want to take bus tours, because I might have a diarrhea attack. I didn't want to take helicopter rides because I couldn't get out if I wanted to. I didn't want to sit up on the balcony of our room because we were on the twenty-second floor. What if I fell? Worse still, what if I jumped? How embarrassing! I often wonder what David saw in me, but I think he must have seen the "me" I am today. He must have known my hidden capabilities; he could see them. He just couldn't find a good reason for my fears. When we returned from Mexico, I tried therapy, but it wasn't the right kind for me. I wanted someone to tell me what was making me suffer, and to help me heal. I wanted to get better, but I seemed to be getting worse and avoiding more. I worried about my health: was I dying of some terrible disease? I worried about my sanity: was I losing my mind? I worried about my spacey feelings and my inability to breathe deeply: would I be able to function?

An Answer to My Prayers

One night, when I was obsessed with scary thoughts, David offered to take me out for dinner to get my mind off myself. I insisted on picking the restaurant and sitting as close to the door as possible. I didn't eat because I didn't want to get an upset stomach and diarrhea. David sat there, enjoying his steak, while I obsessed. What was wrong with me? Would I ever be normal? That night I lay in my living room on the sofa and cried. Was there anyone out there who had what I had and didn't lose their minds or die? Could I be helped? Would I have to live forever with this fear? If so, did I want to keep living? I was afraid to live and afraid to die. It seemed as if there were no answers.

I finally did something I hadn't done in a long time. I prayed out loud. I asked God to please, please help me. "Please God, show me someone who has survived this. Give me an answer. Help me. I promise to help you for the rest of my life." At the time I didn't even know what I was talking about. It just came out of desperation and pain. I had no idea of the immense, lifelong commitment I had just made.

The next morning I was getting ready for work, wondering how I was going to make it through another day. I turned on the TV, an unusual thing for me to do in the mornings. On the *Today Show*, a guest was talking about something called agoraphobia. I half listened because I had understood agoraphobics to be people who couldn't leave their houses. I could. Obviously, that wasn't me. I barely paid any attention to the TV, it was just background, until I heard a vivid description of the panic attacks I called my "things" filtering into my awareness. I sat at the edge of the bed staring at the television, riveted. She was describing a condition called anxiety disorder, and its related panic attacks and fear. I was in awe. She was talking about me. My "things" were panic attacks. "You can be helped," she said in her closing statement. My prayer had been answered.

Wake-Up Call

At that time there wasn't a lot of help or information about anxiety disorder. That's when I took control. I would help myself and find my own answers. I spent months researching and studying. Little did I know I was beginning an awakening process that would change my life forever.

Now I am convinced that I suffered all those years for a reason. I have conquered my anxiety, panic attacks, and phobias. I really believe we go through difficult situations to learn from them and then use what we have learned to help make the world a better place by helping others who are going through similar experiences.

Today I am living a full, exciting, happy, peaceful life. Is my life perfect? Of course not. Do I still worry and have anxiety at times? Yes, but it's different. I used to worry endlessly about pointless things. I used to be anxious lying in bed with no real issue to deal with. I don't do any of that now. When my sister was diagnosed with cancer, I worried and was anxious at the thought of losing her, but it was a *real* issue. Even when the issue is real and anxiety-producing, I control my reactions. You, too, can develop the skills necessary to control your thoughts, which in turn control your reactions. This will keep you from creating the anxiety symptoms.

ONE STEP FORWARD, TWO STEPS BACK

Life is too precious to waste it with worry. Anything worth having takes a considerable amount of effort. One of the most important skills that will support that effort is resilience. Being able to bounce back when things don't go your way. Being able to get up and try again when you fall down. It is important to understand that:

❧**Recovery from anything is usually one step forward, two steps back. Failure is an inevitable part of the path to success.**

Don't be discouraged if you feel in control one day and totally anxious the next. Just as it took time for you to develop your fear and anxiety, it also takes time and patience to overcome them. Unfortunately we are not patient people. We like immediate gratification. But very rarely does anything of great value come quickly or easily. Some of the most rewarding things in my life were having and raising my children, maintaining a strong and healthy marriage, building a multimillion dollar company, and overcoming a severe anxiety problem. Each of them took an immense amount of effort, an extended amount of time, various levels of disappointment, and intermittent feelings of failure and success.

I remember when I was researching anxiety and agoraphobia in my desperate search for answers. I would feel good for a few days and then one bad experience would set me back. I often found myself wondering if recovery and healing were really possible. Would the time ever come when I wouldn't feel neurotic and anxious? Would I ever be "normal" again? To me that was the goal, to go back to feeling normal.

❧ **Let me suggest that you avoid setting a goal to be normal.**

In the first place, there's no such thing. Who's normal? It sounds kind of boring, don't you think? In the second place, would you really want to go back to being who you used to be?

There was a young woman who went through our group who reminded me of how I used to be with my anxiety disorder. One time, when we were talking after a session, she said, "I just wish I could go back to being who I used to be before I got this anxiety disorder. I was independent and I didn't have all these avoidances. I would do almost anything."

"Think back," I suggested, "about who you really 'used to be.' Were you an overreactor? Were you a worrier? Did you limit yourself by your fears and insecurities?"

"Yes," she answered. "I was all of that."

I continued. "Was the old 'you' confident? Secure within yourself? Going after the things you wanted in life?"

"No. That's not who I was."

"Then why would you want to go back to being someone who wasn't secure and happy? The goal is not to go back to who you were. The goal is to be better than you've ever been before!"

She liked that idea and we nodded in agreement.

The Anxiety Excuse

As awful as your anxiety may be, it probably gives you a great excuse not to do things that you know in your heart you would like to do. This is a very difficult realization, but a necessary one. It took me a while to realize that, although it was uncomfortable, I was using my anxiety disorder as a familiar and easy way out. Ask yourself if, perhaps on a subconscious level, your anxiety is keeping you from doing something that feels too challenging to deal with. As long as you stay anxious, you have an excuse not to...end that bad relationship, quit that dead-end job, stand up to that person in your life who takes advantage of you or mistreats you. Sometimes it's easier to stay anxious. At least it's familiar. If you change and take a risk, you may create an uncomfortable situation. But I guarantee you:

❊ **The anxiety of staying stagnant and feeling out of control is much worse than the anxiety of changing and challenging yourself.**

This concept was an eye-opener for me. I was certain I wasn't getting anything out of my anxiety except avoidance and negative feelings. In time, I realized that by recovering, there would no longer be an excuse not to go after my dreams. That was scary because I was afraid of failure. The anxiety gave me a great reason to stay where I was, not to change careers, not to try anything too stressful.

Another example was in my relationships. My anxiety and panic were so frightening and made me feel so insecure, I used them as excuses to stay in unhealthy relationships. What if I couldn't take care of myself or survive on my own? There were several people in my life who were draining me and taking advantage of me. As strong as my desire was to express my feelings, stronger still was my fear of rejection. As a result I became more anxious, which functioned as an excuse not to take the risk. In evaluating my life I saw that, although my anxiety was a wonderful scapegoat, the only person who was being cheated was me. Overcoming anxiety disorder meant freedom. Freedom meant risk, opportunity, challenges, a feeling of being alive. These realizations motivated me toward recovery. Once I had a small taste of freedom from fear, I wanted more. I was motivated to keep going. When you begin to trust yourself to try new things and take some risks, before you know it, you are doing things that you only dreamed about.

There is a secret to healing and getting your life back when you struggle with anxiety or any emotional challenge:

�֍ **You hold the key. You have the power to heal yourself.**

It's a matter of being willing to look deep within for answers and insights. You might feel a little resistant at first and it might even make you slightly more anxious. This is because you know you must change and change is scary. Try to look at some of your scared feelings as excitement. Finally, you are taking control. You are taking action.

Five Techniques Toward Recovery

The process of going from panic to power is a gradual one. As you move through this book I suggest you do the following:

1. **Begin by being compassionate, patient, and gentle with yourself. Stop thinking, saying, and doing things that make you feel bad, anxious, or upset with yourself.**
2. **Give yourself credit for any success. The simple act of buying this book shows that you are ready for change. Praise yourself for even the smallest accomplishments.**
3. **Keep an open mind. No matter who you are or what you've been through, I believe you can be helped. But you must want help. You must want to get better. You must want to take responsibility for yourself, something I'll talk about later in the book.**
4. **Don't overreact to your anxious feelings. Instead of fighting them, listen to them. Are you tired? Are you scaring yourself with your thoughts? Relax and let them pass...and they will.**
5. **Keep a journal. Note when you feel anxious, note when you feel good. Write down what you were doing, who you were with, what you just ate, and what time of day it was. This will help you see if there is a pattern to your anxious episodes. I think you will find that there is.**

If you are someone who has been searching for answers for years, if you feel hopeless, please don't give up. Know you are not alone. There *are* answers. There *is* help. Lots of it. Don't let anyone tell you that you have to learn to live with your anxiety or panic attacks. You don't! Don't worry that you are losing control. You're not. You just feel as if you are. If you're searching for better ways to cope with the challenges of life, if you're looking for increased self-esteem and confidence, you'll find skills in this book to help you.

✤**Life is a fabulous adventure. It wasn't meant to be lived in fear.**

Do you want to conquer panic attacks or get rid of that "fuzzy in the head" feeling? Is it your desire to go back to school or to start your own company? Perhaps you want to overcome a fear of public speaking or conquer a fear of flying. Or maybe you just want to stop your mind from racing with broken obsessive thoughts. I truly believe that things happen for a reason and it is no accident that you are reading this book right now. You are full of possibilities. You are full of your own individual hopes and dreams. You are more ready than ever to take control of your anxiety. Whatever your deepest desires, whatever your secret wishes, read on. Once you overcome your fears, it's all possible.

CHAPTER 2

ANXIETY: WHAT IS IT AND DO YOU HAVE IT?

✤*Fear is conquered by action.*
When we challenge our fears, we defeat them.
When we grapple with our difficulties,
They lose their hold upon us.
When we dare to face the
Things which scare us,
We open the door to freedom.

—AUTHOR UNKNOWN

Dear Lucinda,

I have been suffering with anxiety/panic disorder and agoraphobia for 9 years. I have read 10+ books and have seen 5 psychologists and 3 psychiatrists and doctors. Let's just say I know almost every cardiologist, general practitioner, neurologist and internist in the area. They all confirmed anxiety disorder, told me I was the worst case they had ever seen, and sent me home with a bottle of Xanax. My bathroom cabinet looks like a pharmacy, but because of my fear of medication, I refused to take medications which drove my doctors crazy. I have been in the emergency room so many times, I know all the nurses by name. I have had every test imaginable. My symptoms have been palpitations, tachycardia, headaches and neckaches, numbness in my face, arms and legs, and dizziness. I was so dizzy for 4 months, I couldn't get out of bed. My ears rang, I had choking sensations, I lived with constant fearful thoughts and exhaustion. I was a neat freak and couldn't function without utter perfection.

A few months ago, in the middle of the night, I woke up in a panic. I put the TV on to try to take my mind off my symptoms and I saw your show. I began to cry, which I hadn't done in years, and I ordered your tapes. Well, since that first tape, I have changed and I have begun to take my life back. After all I tried before I found the Midwest Center, I had pretty much given up hope. I am truly grateful to all of you.

Christina

ANXIETY ATTACKS IN DIFFERENT WAYS

I'd like to tell you a few stories.

Susan was nineteen. She worked for a small computer company as a receptionist. She enjoyed her job; she liked her boss. She lived at home with her parents and was engaged to her high school sweetheart. She led a basically sheltered life and by all outward appearances, she was happy and healthy.

One day, something changed. She complained about feeling "sick." She started having trouble dealing with the pressures of a growing company. It became difficult for her to communicate with her boss. She felt nervous sitting at her desk. Her heart would pound for no reason and she was nauseated a lot of the time. She felt "trapped." She started calling in sick, missing work more and more frequently.

Finally, at the request of her parents, she went to the doctor. Nothing was physically wrong. This scared her. The doctor suggested she might be depressed. This scared her more. She was hospitalized. She was put on various antidepressants. This scared her even more.

After returning home from the hospital, she felt embarrassed and frightened. She began to believe that she was unable to cope. She began to avoid going out. She lost her job. She put her wedding plans on hold. Her life was falling apart; she felt completely alone in her suffering. The thought of leaving her parents' home and becoming independent scared her...

Susan was suffering from anxiety.

Daniel was a good-looking guy in his late twenties. He was in sales. He always did everything fast. He talked fast, he walked fast. He said he had to "get his success now" because you never know how long you'll be here or what tomorrow holds. He worried constantly about dying. One night he had severe chest pains. He thought he was having a heart attack and he ended up in the emergency room. They didn't find anything. This happened several times.

Daniel worried about different types of cancer. Beer and wine calmed him down and helped him stop worrying. He developed a drinking problem. He developed marital problems. He knew he needed help but he felt ashamed to talk about his fear...

Daniel was suffering from anxiety.

*   *   *

Laura was a beautiful woman. She had everything: a great husband, a wonderful home, healthy, loving children. But Laura always felt dissatisfied. She always thought she was missing something.

She blamed her unhappiness on her husband and her children. She said she had given up her life for them. She was angry and yelled often. She threatened to leave. She worried about her mood swings and her uncontrollable anger. She cried when she was alone, wondering why she couldn't just be happy and satisfied...

Laura suffered with anxiety.

Joan had three children under the age of seven. She was a good mother, staying home with her kids most of the time. But she began to have scary thoughts about hurting them. She didn't tell anyone; she was too ashamed. She began to worry about being alone with her children. She began to worry about her own sanity. She started having trouble sleeping. She would lie in bed, wide awake, and worry about not getting enough sleep. She felt guilty and feared that she was a terrible mother. And yet, she was a wonderful mother.

When she finally opened up to her husband, crying and telling him about her obsessive thoughts, he became angry. He told her to stop doing this to herself. He told her she was scaring herself. He told her she was perfectly capable of just stopping it. This made her feel more guilty. She thought about her father who had committed suicide. She worried constantly that she might take her own life. She felt imprisoned...

Joan's captor was anxiety.

Michael was an emergency room physician. He was very smart, skilled, and talented. He loved his job, got along with his colleagues, and was good with his patients. But he had dizzy feelings in the emergency room. He would sometimes feel strange and spacey for hours at a time. He couldn't tell his colleagues how he felt for fear of losing his job. He didn't know where to turn for help. He felt he should have been able to help himself. After all, he was a doctor...

Michael's problem was anxiety.

Lucinda was outgoing. She appeared strong and confident. But she worried. She worried about her future; she worried about her past. She worried about being liked, about fitting in, and being good enough. She developed eating problems. She felt nauseated at the thought of food. She developed irritable bowel syndrome. She lost weight and became very thin.

Eventually she couldn't drive, fly, or even talk on the phone comfortably. She began to plan all her social activities around her inability to move independently. She started having panic attacks whenever she felt she was in a situation where she couldn't control her comings and goings. Her life had begun to control her...

Lucinda was a prisoner to her own anxiety.

Lucinda was me. I had anxiety disorder. I was the child who had scary dreams and scary thoughts. In my adolescence, I always felt I was different. During my teenage years, I avoided doing a lot of things the other kids did, and I didn't understand why. I only knew that there was something awfully wrong with me and I was very frightened most of the time. As a young adult in my early twenties, my anxiety was in full swing, manifesting in the form of constant panic attacks, ongoing feelings of spaceyness, along with feelings of fear and insecurity. By this time, irritable bowel syndrome was a major problem.

Anticipation Is Far Worse Than Reality

I remember when one of my worst fears became a reality. It's a funny little story but I know some of you will relate! I had attended a conference with a colleague of mine and we decided to share a hotel room. I was apprehensive about rooming with anyone, especially a colleague. "What if I have a diarrhea attack?" I thought, packing my trusty bottle of Pepto Bismol, just in case.

After attending a sumptuous banquet, we returned to our room. It was very quiet in the early hours of the morning as we lay in our beds, talking about the night's events. All of a sudden, the all too familiar rumblings in my stomach began. My mind raced with anticipation. "Oh, my Gosh! I'm about to have an attack. It's so quiet in here. She'll hear me." I shut down, turned my focus inward, anticipating the worst, creating more symptoms. She just kept talking. I got up and headed for the bathroom. She followed me without a break in her conversation. I went into the bathroom and shut the door. She sat down outside the door and continued to talk.

It appeared that she never noticed what was happening in the bathroom. And if she did, she didn't care. Why should she have cared? She's never had diarrhea? This was a great example of an intense fear coming true, but not being anywhere near as bad as the anticipation. As a matter of fact, the anticipation of things is almost always worse than the event itself. And how often do we worry about things that never happen at all?

My biggest fears were about going insane and losing control. My second biggest fears were about illness and death. I also worried about strange things like the occult and the end of the world. I was consumed with "What is wrong with me?" and other scary thoughts.

In spite of all my suffering and avoidance, I can honestly

say now that I'm glad I had anxiety disorder. It was a curse, but it was a blessing as well. It was terrifically painful, but it forced me to grow up. It forced me to acquire coping skills that the average person could definitely use, but will probably never be in enough pain to investigate. My disorder gave me insight and taught me how not to be an overreactor. Since the day that I defined my anxiety and went to work to heal it, my life has been so fulfilling. Today, I'm not afraid to take chances and I'm excited about living. I stay in the present moment instead of the past or the future. I am happy and living a peaceful life. And you can do as well as I have done.

DEFINING ANXIETY

Let's begin with a dictionary definition: "Anxiety is a painful or apprehensive uneasiness of mind usually over an impending or anticipated ill. It is a fearful concern or interest, marked by physiological signs (as sweating, tension or increased pulse), by doubt concerning the reality and nature of the threat, and by self-doubt of one's capacity to cope with it."

Everyone has anxiety. It is a natural part of life. When it reaches the level where it disrupts your lifestyle, it becomes a disorder. There are four factors one must consider when discussing anxiety disorder.

Genetics

Anxiety disorder tends to run in families. This means you might have a mother, father, grandparent, or sibling with anxiety problems. Did you grow up with someone who had problems with anxiety and depression? Did someone in your family suffer silently with panic and obsessive thoughts? Did they use "nerve pills" or alcohol to self-medicate?

I have discovered that alcoholism does not create anxiety. My father didn't become anxious because he abused alcohol. In fact, it's the other way around; he abused alcohol because he was anxious and depressed. He was probably genetically prone to anxiety and alcoholism. Additionally, he went through a difficult childhood, which made him environmentally prone to anxiety and depression. He used alcohol to self-medicate. When he finally went to the doctor, he was prescribed Valium, commonly used back then. This contributed to a combined problem of drug and alcohol abuse.

What does it mean if you have a relative who was prone to problems with anxiety or nervousness or depression? Actually, it's more important in diagnosis than in treatment. The recovery process is the same whether the cause is your genetic makeup or if your anxiety occurs spontaneously. If you are genetically prone to anxiety or depression or alcoholism, it doesn't mean that you will end up with a disorder, so don't be frightened by it. It simply means that you should be aware of it, especially if you start experiencing symptoms.

Environment

Environment plays a significant role in anxiety disorders. Did you have a mother who constantly worried? Did your parents expect you always to be perfect? Did you grow up with strict religious beliefs? Was your family environment dysfunctional? Was there any separation from a significant person in your life as a child? It can be helpful to realize that some of these environmental situations could create anxious attitudes and a tendency toward problems with anxiety and depression. But if you shift the responsibility of your anxiety to a past experience or another person by using blame, it can work against you. When you say to yourself, "I had a difficult childhood," or "This was in my background," or possibly, "He is why I have this problem," it doesn't make you feel better.

Subconsciously, you might use it to justify your problem, which will prevent you from getting better. Taking responsibility for how you feel and where you are in your life is a big part of the recovery process, which we will discuss in greater detail later in the book.

Biochemistry

It's a common belief that people with anxiety disorder have excessive catecholamine activity. This means that they are prone to feelings of hypersensitivity and nervousness. It is also concluded that these people have less endorphin activity.

I don't believe that anxiety is solely a biochemical imbalance that must be handled with medication. In fact, some medications can make your symptoms worse. Since endorphins help us control the way we think and respond, we are personally capable of creating more endorphins and of reducing our catecholamine activity.

We'll learn more about the roles of biochemistry and medication in a future chapter. We'll also cover personality traits, one of my favorite and most important topics. For now, it's important to understand that the overreacting, negative way we think causes most of our anxiety.

Personality Traits

Anxious people share certain types of personality traits which are responsible for a good deal of their anxiety. Such people are often analytical worriers who dwell on things and obsess about their fears. They want things to be a certain way and have extremely high expectations. As a result, they are often disappointed and anxious. Winning the approval of others is important to them, and at all costs they must appear to be in control. Anticipation and dread of negative events are a large part of their thought process, and at the smallest threat of a challenge, they tend to overreact.

It is this type of thinking and reacting that creates the biochemical response which in turn creates anxiety. It is impossible to recover until you are willing to take a serious look at your specific personality traits, and be willing to change them. When you change the way you think, you change the way you respond and react. As a result, you change the biochemical reaction which will minimize and eventually prevent the anxiety.

SYMPTOMS, FEARS, AND CONCERNS

There are a host of physical symptoms associated with anxiety disorder. Some of the more common symptoms would include:

- strong episodes of anxiousness and panicky feelings
- racing heart and chest discomfort
- dizziness or lightheadedness
- feelings of bewilderment and unreality
- inner nervousness
- scary, uncontrollable thoughts
- nausea, upset stomach, diarrhea
- hot and cold flashes
- numbness or strange aches and pains, muscle tension
- feelings of depression and hopelessness

- restless feelings, insomnia, or sleeping too much
- difficulty in breathing (hyperventilation)
- uncontrollable bouts of anger

People who suffer with anxiety disorder tend to worry and obsess about some or all of the following:

- having a heart attack
- going insane
- losing control
- embarrassment
- death
- illness
- hurting themselves or someone else
- fainting
- difficulty in breathing

The irony here is that these fears actually create the above symptoms and the above symptoms can create these fears. It is a vicious cycle.

Mental Illness vs. Emotional Disorder

One of the most important points to keep in mind is this:

❧ **Anxiety is not a mental illness.**

With mental disorders like schizophrenia or manic-depression, the problem is chemical and biological, often creating an extremely distorted view of reality. Typically these illnesses must be treated with medication, often for the entire span of a person's life.

The mere mention of mental illness seems to bring up fear and judgment, so I would like to point out that there is a stigma attached to mental illness that desperately needs to be eradicated. Mental illness is not something to be afraid of or ashamed of. We have come far in our ability to help people with mental illness. We must understand that every case is unique, that there are different levels of mental illness, and that many people can live normal lives with the help of therapy and medication.

In our clinic, we categorize anxiety as an emotional disorder. One of the main differences between anxiety disorder and mental illness is that anxiety often can be treated successfully with self-help methods and without anti-anxiety medication. The symptoms come and go; they are not consistent, although they are usually recurring. Anxiety disorder is characterized by fearful feelings without any reality-based danger, an emotional state of worry or deep concern. The main differentiating element between mental illness and an anxiety disorder is that you can recover completely from anxiety, often without the use of long-term medication.

The *Diagnostic and Statistical Manual of Psychiatric Disorders* (DSM) divides anxiety into various categories, including post-traumatic stress disorder, panic disorder, obsessive/compulsive disorder, generalized anxiety disorder, and agoraphobia. It further defines each anxiety disorder as a mental disorder.

As stated earlier, I don't consider anxiety a mental illness. Also, I believe that the various categories overlap; they are coexisting. For example, during our twelve years of providing ongoing group therapy sessions at the Midwest Center, we have found the following to be true:

• **Most people who experience anxiety are obsessive thinkers but are not necessarily compulsive.**

When you think obsessively you get one thought in your mind and dwell on it over and over again. When you have compulsive behaviors, you may do something over and over such as washing your hands or checking things such as the locks on the doors. You might be compulsive about germs or disease, feeling the need to wipe doorknobs or to keep on washing things.

• **Many who experience agoraphobia also experience panic attacks, although they may not think so.**

Agoraphobia is most simply defined as the fear of being in public places. Panic attacks are strong episodes of anxiety accompanied by various body symptoms like heart palpitations, nervousness, dizziness, and difficulty in breathing. During a panic attack, there is usually an urgency to "get out" and go somewhere that you might feel safe.

• **Most people who suffer from anxiety disorder can trace the onset back to some stressful event, which would also be categorized as post-traumatic stress disorder.**

Post-traumatic stress disorder is anxiety brought on by some type of stressful event in a person's life. Sometimes it is accompanied by recurring bad dreams or flashbacks.

• **Almost everyone with any type of anxiety problem experiences generalized anxiety.**

This is when anxiety is high, although not at the panic stage. It is there for no apparent reason. You feel a sense of inner nervousness and anticipation. This feeling can last for hours and is often accompanied by feelings of spaceyness, bewilderment, and confusion.

In short, many people experience some of the symptoms in each category. This does not pose additional healing problems because all symptoms are treated in much the same way: by behavioral/cognitive restructuring and gradual exposure. You learn how to think, behave, react, and respond differently. Then, once you have some solid insight about your problems and have incorporated good coping skills, you gradually expose yourself to your fears.

Please don't try to do this until you have reprogrammed yourself. You can get in the car and attempt to drive on a highway you've been avoiding, but unless you understand why you have the fear of driving on the highway, what causes it, how to respond to it and work through it, you could add more anxiety to an already uncomfortable situation.

- Gain an understanding of your fears and restructure your thoughts and reactions.
- Grasp the coping skills.
- Test out your skills by doing the activity you've been avoiding.

As you read through this book and gain new insights, you may observe positive behavioral and thought changes in your life, but until you get on that plane, you will not overcome your fear of flying. Get the insight, develop the skills, and then go out and face your fears with some effective coping techniques. You can't help but win.

For many years, people with severe anxiety disorder were hospitalized. Fortunately, we have educated ourselves enough to understand that, although it is believed that anxiety has caused more suffering in the world than any other disorder, hospitalization is not necessary for most people.

Some hospitals do offer inpatient treatment programs specializing in anxiety disorder that can be beneficial and effective. Every person's needs are unique, so if hospitalization is an option you are considering, I strongly suggest you talk with your doctor and therapist. Look into inpatient programs that specialize in anxiety disorder, but I would suggest you also consider outpatient options before making your choice. Take a little time to decide. Your impatience to "get better fast" is common and understandable, but recovery comes in its own time.

Typically, hospitalization is appropriate when anxiety is accompanied by moderate to severe depression, a condition which is often treated with medication. The patient is hospitalized to receive therapy and to be under observation during their introduction to various medications until he or she stabilizes. If you feel you may have a problem with depression, talk with your doctor. There are various written tests your doctor can offer which will provide you with a fairly reliable diagnosis.

When anxiety is your main problem, depression is often a secondary problem. People who have anxiety disorder are typically independent people who feel "out of control" of their fears and feelings. They begin to feel dependent. As a result, they become depressed. Occasionally, when you have conquered your fears and anxiety, you continue to feel symptoms of depression. In this case, an antidepressant might be useful. If this is the case for you, along with the material we will be presenting in Chapter 12, please discuss depression with your doctor.

✤ Anxiety is an emotion. You can control it.

Everyone experiences anxiety to varying degrees, so you'll be relieved to know that you have something that everyone else has. What you do with your anxiety determines whether you will keep it under control or let it control you. Let's take a look at the stimulant response that anxiety causes in our brains to understand better how an anxious episode erupts.

There are two types of anxiety. The first type is external.

It's produced by outside circumstances: a dramatic television show, sitting in a traffic jam and worrying about being late for work, an argument with a spouse, or an anxious moment in the morning when you wake up. If someone broke into your house, you'd be nervous and frightened, wondering if you or your family were going to be hurt, and frightened about what else might happen. These are all examples of situations that produce anxiety, a normal reaction that the average person would have.

The second type of anxiety is internal. That is to say, it's internally generated. It begins with a thought. Just a simple thought. A "what-if" thought that creates a chain of more scary thoughts. What if my husband doesn't like what I said? What if he becomes so angry, he won't forgive me? What if he leaves me? What if I'm all alone and can't take care of myself? What if I go crazy and there's no one there to help me? What if I cry until I can't breathe? What if I die?

One upsetting thought creates the next. Pretty soon, you are like a hamster on a treadmill, going round and round in circles, getting nowhere, feeling more frustrated all the time.

What if I hurt her feelings?
What if she doesn't like me?
What if I get sick?
What if I'm late to work this morning?
What if I lose control while I'm driving?
What if my boss gets mad at me?
What if I lose my job?
What if I stand up and scream on the plane?
What if my heart keeps pounding so hard?
What if I have a heart attack?
What if the plane crashes?
What if I do something to embarrass myself?

You can step off the wheel any time you want. Remember, anxiety is not a monster: it is not some severe illness that requires lifelong medication. It is self-induced. We think the worst and then our thoughts become the generator of this biochemical reaction in our bodies. It is encouraging to know that we are not victims, that anxiety doesn't just happen to us, that most often we create it; therefore, we can control it. Once we realize that not only do we cause it, but we also keep regenerating the cycle of fear, we will also understand the most important step in the healing process.

❀**Your anxiety is under your control. You created the negative thoughts, therefore, you can stop them.**

The Adrenaline Response

Whatever the initial cause, whether it comes from inside or out, a sudden moment of anxiety automatically sends a signal to our brain. An alarm system has been activated and a hormone called adrenaline is secreted. That's how it all starts. Our nervous system has been warned that something is wrong, that danger is present or possible. Cortisol is secreted. Then, these stimulants rapidly course through the body.

This biochemical response is not a malfunction of the central nervous system. Quite the contrary. It is a part of our survival mechanism. For example, if you were at the supermarket and a man held a gun to your head, that's external and that's real. Your body would immediately respond by registering trouble. Then boom! Adrenaline and cortisol would start racing through your body. The central nervous system is hypersensitive; when it receives these stimulants, it reacts with what we call the "flight or fight" response. It is as if our own internal armed forces have been called to attention. You're ready to defend yourself or run away as fast as you can. All systems are prepared for survival, whatever that means in a particular situation. This is an appropriate response from a healthy, functioning system trying to protect itself.

When we get worked up by a thought in our mind, the same automatic response happens. In this case, the anxiety is all in the mind, generated by the mind. Our heart begins to pump faster, transporting oxygen to the muscles in the legs and arms. The stomach—a vulnerable center which in combat would need protection—contracts as blood moves swiftly away from it. You get a chronically upset stomach, nausea, or cramping and you think "What if I have stomach cancer?" Blood rushes into the arms and legs and out of the hands and feet, the protruding limbs which are also vulnerable to being injured. Your fingers and toes become cold. They tingle and you think "What if I have multiple sclerosis?" Your heart pounds so hard, you think "What if I'm having a heart attack?" The blood rushes out of your head causing dizziness and you think "What if I have a brain tumor?" There is nothing to be done with your overstimulated system, so it turns in on itself. You are now just a step away from panic. Do you see what we do to ourselves?

Bewilderment: A Healthy Response

I remember a time when that feeling of bewilderment overtook me. David and I were having a party. My adrenaline was running rampant; I was in my usual anticipation mode, filled with expectations and doubts about the food, the music, and my abilities as a hostess. Everything had to be perfect: the house, my clothes, the appetizers, my husband's appearance. Everything. If I was so concerned, wouldn't you think I would have had the event catered or, at the very least, picked up something already prepared to relieve the pressure? But no. I had to do it all myself. Needless to say, by the end of the day's preparations, I was exhausted. I was at the point of just wanting to skip the whole thing; I was absolutely dreading it. I had worn myself out.

One of the guests, Dawn, arrived early, and to my dismay, she decided to stand in the kitchen and talk to me while I finished preparing the food. I was feeling so spacey, so fuzzy in the head, that I couldn't hear a word she was saying. I was so spaced out, I picked up the Betty Crocker cookbook and unconsciously stuck it in the refrigerator! A few minutes later, I noticed that my cookbook was missing. Dawn helped me look for it. We couldn't seem to find it, so we both gave up the search, certain it had disappeared into thin air. When I opened the refrigerator a few minutes later and saw the cookbook on the middle shelf, I was devastated. "Oh, no!" I thought. "How did I do that? What will Dawn think?" I pulled it out quickly, laid it on the counter, and waited for her to respond. She didn't. Instead, she kept right on talking and never even noticed. She was too caught up in her conversation to notice. When I was in recovery and finally had stopped resisting my spacey feelings, allowed myself to have them and floated with them, they went away much faster.

When anxiety strikes, many people feel bewildered or disoriented, and they think they're losing their minds. Our staff psychologist at the Midwest Center, Dr. Jim Boldus, tells us that bewilderment is a healthy mechanism that can actually help us cope. "For someone with excessive anxiety or a condition of agoraphobia," he says, "bewilderment is a healthy response. Think of it as the mind's way of taking a break from the emotional overload. When someone has been through a traumatic event, a mild form of shock takes over. This is good; the system needs to shut down because it can't comprehend all that is bombarding the senses. The same thing happens with overwhelming anxiety. It's the body's way of taking care of itself." This spacey, fuzzy feeling is simply your mind's way of taking a mini-vacation.

This "fuzzy in the head" feeling can last several hours, making it difficult to concentrate, but it won't hurt you. Remember, it's only an adrenaline response. Adrenaline always stabilizes. You *will* feel "normal" again. The best thing to do when you recognize these feelings of confusion or fuzziness is to make light of them. Try to float with the feelings. Accept them and let yourself be. Tell yourself, "This is natural. This is a healthy response and my body is taking care of me." Although it may seem that you won't be able to function, you actually will. You are not losing your mind. You are not crazy. The bewildered feelings will go away. Try to think about something positive. When you focus on the fear, you will only create more adrenaline, and cortisol, which will in turn produce more body symptoms and more confusion. I know the cycle well. Bewilderment was one of my most consistent symptoms, but besides scaring me, it never hurt me physically.

Health Obsessions

When a flood of adrenaline hits the limbic system of the brain, we feel intense terror. The thinking part of our brain reacts; it begins to look for something to substantiate the terror. If it finds nothing on the outside, we turn inward and start to question the symptoms. We often run from doctor to doctor, searching for answers and reassurance. This is a natural reaction; something feels wrong and we want to fix it. In fact, seeing a doctor is the right course of action. At the onset of pain, I would strongly suggest that you have a complete physical checkup to rule out any physical causes for your symptoms.

Afraid you might find something? Afraid you might not? I understand. That's exactly how I felt, but believe me, the ongoing misery of obsessing over your health is much worse than the brief anxiety you will experience as a result of deciding to have a checkup. You can drive yourself into a panic attack with constant worry about a heart problem, cancer, a brain tumor, mental illness, and so on and so on. Chances are, you'll be fine. And if there is something wrong, at least you'll know and you can take steps to begin to deal with it. It is much more likely that you will come up with a clean bill of health. Your mind will be put to rest and then you can focus on overcoming the real problem: your anxiety.

YOUR PERSONAL ANXIETY EVALUATION

If you have anxiety—and who doesn't—you needn't label yourself agoraphobic or someone with panic disorder. Whether anxiety plays a major or minor role in your life, you will benefit from taking control of it. Whatever degree of discomfort you have, it will be worthwhile to take steps to gain control of your life and make it better.

Let's do an experiment to discover your anxiety levels. Choose which of the following situations and events are uncomfortable for you due to your specific anxiety symptoms. Beside each, on a scale of 1 to 3, indicate how often you would avoid (1. never; 2. sometimes; 3. often) and how much anxiety you would feel (1. minimum; 2. moderate; 3. extreme) if you participated. If there is a particular situation or event that bothers you that is not listed, please feel free to add it at the bottom.

Event	Level of Avoidance	Level of Anxiety
1. Shopping in stores		
2. Eating in restaurants		
3. Eating in front of people		
4. Writing checks		
5. Driving		
6. Traveling distances		
7. Standing in lines		
8. Heights		
9. Bridges		
10. Sitting in meetings		
11. Enclosed areas		
12. Going to church		
13. Socializing with people		
14. Flying		
15. Talking in front of others		
16. Crowded areas		
17. Being alone		
18. Other		

Choose which body symptoms you experience during an anxious period.

( ) racing heart/chest discomfort
( ) trembling/nervousness
( ) dizziness
( ) feeling confused and bewildered
( ) diarrhea
( ) shortness of breath
( ) numbness in various parts of body
( ) feelings of fatigue and depression

( ) nausea
( ) hot or cold flashes
( ) muscle tension
( ) headaches
( ) insomnia/sleeping too much
( ) restless feelings
( ) strange thoughts
( ) feelings of helplessness

( ) unexplainable panicky   ( ) uncontrollable bouts of anger
feelings

This has not been a test; rather it is a self-evaluation. Now that you have filled out this form, take some time to review it. What do you notice about yourself? Is your anxiety disrupting the flow of your life? Did any of your answers surprise you? Do you see areas you'd like to change but you just don't know how? There is a way and you can do it.

This Book Is for Everyone

You may be thinking, "Gee, I'm not that bad. I don't avoid doing things. I can drive, fly, and function. I don't have panic attacks. I just get nervous and stressed out. I just worry and can't sleep." If these are your thoughts, then this book is for you. Or if you think you have read it all, done it all, been to all the doctors, therapists, and psychiatrists for years and are still on your medications, this book is for you, too. You're probably in the same state that I was in: feeling uncertain, discouraged, disappointed, and helpless. You may feel as if no one understands and there's no hope for you.

I'm here to say that I *do* understand. I've been there. Don't give up. There is help. You aren't weird or crazy and most importantly, you are not alone. You may have spent lots of time and money and you're still suffering.

❅ **You've been trying to treat the symptoms of your problem, but not the cause.**

Please continue to read. You *can* recover if you will suspend your analytical behavior and skepticism for just a little while. This is a big part of the problem, but after what we've been through and how long we've looked for help, who can blame us for being skeptical? Fortunately, many skeptical people have strong determination and, therefore, will experience great results. Why shouldn't you be one of them?

CHAPTER 3

WHERE DO YOU RUN WHEN PANIC ATTACKS?

❋ You gain strength, courage, and confidence by every experience in which you really stop to look fear in the face... The danger lies in refusing to face the fear, in not daring to come to grips with it... You must make yourself succeed every time. You must do the thing you think you cannot do.

—ELEANOR ROOSEVELT

Many people are uncomfortable flying. Even people who don't have anxiety disorder sometimes dread it, especially on turbulent flights. People with anxiety disorder are often uncomfortable with all types of transportation, not just flying. Why? It's simple. They aren't in control, of the vehicle, their fears, their ability to get off or to get out. I remember a young woman who was at one of my seminars saying, "It's a control thing, Lucinda. If I could just fly the plane, I think I'd be okay!"

It was the same thing for me. As my anxiety increased, my ability to travel comfortably decreased. The mere thought of getting on a plane, a train, or a boat made me anxious. I would start anticipating my anxiety days before I left for the trip. I remember a time David and I had made plans to take the train from Detroit to Toronto. I was alone in the apartment packing and I thought, "How can I be trapped in a train for six hours? What if I freak out and do something embarrassing?" The more I thought about it, the more anxious I felt.

As I moved around the apartment, I felt as if I wasn't even in my body. I was somewhere else, disoriented, confused, spacey. The walls were closing in on me. All I was doing was packing. What was the big deal? I basically knew what I wanted to take with me, but making the smallest decision became overwhelming. The brown belt or the black? I couldn't understand why it mattered so much, but each choice in front of me seemed too difficult to make.

This was supposed to be a simple pleasure trip. I was anticipating a short train ride. Why was I so nervous? Why was I so afraid? For me, anticipating was the operative word. In my mind, I was already on the train, and although I wanted to go on the trip, I was also dreading it. My heart was racing at ninety miles an hour. The adrenaline was pumping. I couldn't catch my breath. My palms were sweating. My stomach was churning. "How am I ever going to take a six-hour train trip through the countryside without being able to get off when I want? What if I lose control? I can't do it!"

I wasn't on the train yet and I was already out of control. I was terribly confused and upset. I desperately wanted to go, to participate in the fun that David wanted to share with me. How I wished I could just relax and enjoy getting ready for the trip, like a "normal" person. Why was I feeling so afraid and apprehensive? Maybe I had a real reason. Maybe something terrible was about to happen. Maybe I just shouldn't go.

When David arrived, he immediately sensed my discomfort. He sat beside me and I began describing my feelings. "Something's wrong with me," I told him when I had finished talking about my spaced-out sensations. "Have you ever felt this way? Have you ever felt like your heart was pounding so hard, it was going to pop through your chest? Did you ever think you were going to lose your mind for no good reason?" Please say yes, I thought, so I can know I'm not the only one and I'm not crazy.

"No, Lucinda. I've never felt that way."

My stomach sank. "Well, if you haven't, then I guess I'm losing my mind. I must really be strange."

I wasn't. I was having a panic attack, generated by anticipating a situation where I wouldn't have control.

Somehow, I managed to get on the train. My mind, which already had been obsessing, got steadily worse. I was completely in the past and the future, not at all in the present moment. I was so busy obsessing, I might as well have stayed home.

I tried to look out the window to enjoy the scenery, but my anxiety was so all-absorbing I couldn't see anything. I evaluated my situation. Here I was, on this wonderful train trip that I had been looking forward to. Cruising across the countryside, alone with David, Mr. "Nothing Matters, Everything Is Great Just As It Is." He was laughing, enjoying himself, talking to people.

But not me. I was sitting there, obsessing. "If I have to, how can I stop this train? Could I pull that cord? Would anybody notice that I was the one who did it? How far is the next town? I wonder if they have a hospital?" I stared out the window, but I wasn't admiring the greenery or the sky. I was eyeing every street sign, hoping that they might indicate our approach to a town that would be large enough to have a decent hospital with a staff psychiatrist. It wasn't that I needed one right then. I didn't. But I might need one in a few minutes. You just never knew what might happen next. My heart was racing. The adrenaline was pumping. I couldn't breathe. My stomach was doing cartwheels. My mind was crowded with broken, worrisome thoughts. I was sure I was losing my mind. I wasn't. I was having another panic attack.

Somehow, I got through the train ride. We were finally in Toronto. We arrived at the hotel and checked in. Now maybe I could relax and enjoy my vacation. I knew David must have been hoping for that, too, but unfortunately, I hadn't left my mind on the train. It was right there with me in the hotel lobby. They handed us our room key and the nightmare continued.

"The thirty-third floor?" I whispered to David. "I can't stay on the thirty-third floor. Why do we have to be up so high?" David tried to reassure me but I was filled with fear and anxiety. After an anxious elevator ride, we checked into our room. David was excited and ready to see the sights. I was ready to go home. But I wasn't ready to get back on the train! A no-win situation. We headed out to the city and walked toward the harbor. My breathing got a little bit easier.

David took my hand, hopeful that maybe we could start having a good time. I was so anxious and self-absorbed, it hadn't entered my mind that I might be spoiling David's vacation. "Honey, let's go on a boat ride," he suggested.

"Oh, no," I thought to myself. "What if my irritable bowel syndrome kicks in while we're out on the boat? There's no bathroom. What'll I do? I better stay on safe, dry land."

"I really don't feel like taking a boat ride right now," I told David.

"Okay. I'll go and you stay here and shop," David offered, slightly disappointed but willing to go without me.

"No! Don't go," I pleaded. I couldn't stay behind. What

if I were all alone and I lost my mind and no one was there to help me? But I couldn't go on the boat, either. Another no-win situation, a vicious cycle where nothing felt safe. My heart was pounding. I felt spacey and anxious. The adrenaline was in full force. I was sure I was losing my mind already.

I wasn't. I was having another panic attack.

YOU CREATE YOUR PANIC ATTACKS

Where does it all start? What causes a panic attack? In the case of my so-called vacation to Toronto, what transformed an intended pleasure trip into a constant nightmare?

The trip didn't cause it. I had wanted to go; I had even arranged it. Nobody was making me go.

The train didn't cause it. It was a perfectly safe train, chugging along a beautiful countryside.

The hotel didn't cause it. It was a four star hotel with a good staff and luxurious, spacious rooms.

The boat didn't cause it. It was just a plain old ferryboat, promising to float gently down the harbor.

I caused it. Before the trip even began. I did it with my mind, with anticipatory obsessing. With my "what-if" thoughts. With my unwillingness to stay in the present as I projected first into the past and then into the future. I see it as a three-part process.

1. I was obsessively anticipating.
2. My thoughts created body symptoms.
3. I was in fear of losing control.

When I was by myself, pacing around that apartment, anticipating a trip that would place me in a situation I couldn't control, I created an adrenaline response in my body. I was busy telling myself, mostly on a subconscious level, that there was something to be afraid of. The automatic adrenaline response kicked in and I started having symptoms. My heart pounded and I felt intense fear. I couldn't calm down. The awful, spacey feeling of confusion was clouding my head. My mind responded by registering, "Something is wrong!" Then adrenaline started racing through my body. I was too anxious to focus on anything. Cold sweats and feelings of impending doom catapulted me from straightforward anxiety into the next stage of fear: panic.

It began with internal negative dialogue, the type of thinking that's a sure road to a panic attack. I had a bad case of the "what-ifs." "What if I get on the train and I need to get off? What if I can't catch my breath? What if I embarrass myself? What if I can't stop the train?" I went through my usual litany of fears, creating the second stage of anxiety. Then came thoughts like, "What's wrong with me? Am I going crazy? Am I going to die? Am I going to lose control? Where can I run to get help?"

The cycle progressed, building on itself, until I was so far into it, I had no idea how to get out. I didn't even know that getting out was an option. As I paced the apartment with the walls closing in, my thoughts intensified. My focus was no longer on the trip. Now my focus was on my body symptoms and my scary thoughts. I could see myself being checked into a mental institution, with all the elements of personal control being taken away: straitjackets, heavy medications, inability to communicate. Under the intensity of these ideas and images, my body released ten times the amount of cortisol and adrenaline. The somewhat anxious thoughts that had been intermittently breezing through my head had become nonstop. Increasing in intensity, they became a virtual hurricane, spinning out of control.

At this point of fear escalation, men and women often tend to have slightly different fear fantasies. Typically, men fear they are going to have a heart attack, and women worry they are going to lose control of their minds. Both men and women worry that they will embarrass themselves by doing something foolish or strange. For some people, it overlaps; they fear all of it. Whatever your particular manifestation of fear, you are not only afraid of the original situation that caused you to worry. Your physical symptoms scare you even more.

❊**The past or future event that triggered the anxiety has moved into the background. Now you are afraid of the fear itself; your very survival is in question.**

Your mind turns inward. It's out of control, spinning along in a cycle of fear. It can think only the worst. "This is it! I'm in deep trouble now. What if I have a heart attack? What if I die?"

You no longer feel that you're in control, and in fact you're not. The fear has taken over. If you allow it to reach this point, it has built up so much momentum, you might as well give it a name like "Hurricane Hopeless" and just wait for it to blow over. But wouldn't you rather catch it before it takes you on its tortuous ride? You can. At the end of this chapter and in subsequent chapters, you will receive guidance in how to work with your anxious thoughts to prevent panic attacks from ever happening. You will learn to control your anxiety rather than allowing it to control you.

Some people have panic attacks daily, others have one or two a month, and still others have only one or two over the span of their lives. Panic attacks aren't always easy to recognize or explain. In fact, many people don't even realize they're having one. Instead, they think they're sick, having a heart attack, losing their minds, or even dying. Most often, however, our biggest concern is not about dying. Rather, it is about embarrassment. "Will anyone notice? What will people think? Will I do something foolish to embarrass myself or anybody else?"

In one of our groups at the Center, a man spoke about his fear of heights; he was afraid he'd jump off a balcony.

"So you're afraid you'll die?" I asked him.

"Oh no," he said. "What would people think?"

Because we're so afraid and ashamed of our panic attacks, we often try to tell ourselves that we aren't having one. This very denial is what allows the attack to escalate to a point where we can't do anything about it. But the sooner we recognize the onset of a panic attack, the sooner we can begin working to minimize it. Symptoms, although they differ, are perfectly obvious. If we would only look within, if we were willing to accept what was happening, we would be able to quickly recognize when we were moving toward or beginning a panic attack and subsequently prevent the continuation of the cycle of fear/symptoms/more fear, etc.

Random Panic Attacks

Many people describe their panic attacks as having no apparent external cause. That is because most panic attacks are caused exclusively by internally generated anxiety. Here are some examples:

John was a big man, six foot two, 250 pounds. He managed an auto parts store. He built his own house by the lake. John loved to hunt, cut wood, and fish with his two sons.

John started having strange feelings that seemed to come out of the blue. He would be standing behind the counter at work and suddenly feel nervous. He would get panicky and his heart would beat very fast. He was afraid that people might notice his nervousness. He was afraid he was having a heart attack. He ended up in the emergency room several times. He went through a battery of unpleasant tests. They all came back negative.

John started avoiding hunting and fishing with his sons. He also avoided riding to work with his neighbor. He just couldn't be a passenger in the car. Sometimes, he left work early because of his unmanageable feelings.

John was having panic attacks.

Ann was in her fifties. She had always considered herself easygoing and calm. One day, on the way home from a visit with a friend, she began to feel spacey in her car. She got scared; she felt her heart pounding and couldn't breathe. She pulled over and called her husband. He met her and followed her home.

Ann was so afraid of this happening again, she began to avoid driving distances. One day in church, the spacey feelings returned. Her breathing became shallow. She felt out of control and was afraid she would do something foolish and embarrass herself. She wanted to get up and leave, but she didn't want to be noticed.

She began to avoid going anywhere she thought she might have these frightening feelings: the grocery store, restaurants, movie theaters...

Ann was a prisoner to panic attacks.

Lauren was eight years old. She would get up on a school-day filled with fear. She didn't know why. She complained to her mother about stomachaches and headaches. She cried and refused to go to school.

Her mother couldn't understand what was wrong. She

took Lauren to various doctors, hoping for insight and some answers. She wondered if something had happened at school. She wondered if she had done something to cause her daughter's fearful feelings. She hadn't.

Lauren's symptoms got worse. The school began to wonder if she had problems at home. She didn't. Nobody knew what to do; everybody was looking for someone to blame. There wasn't anyone to blame...

Lauren's "problems" were panic attacks.

Children Have Panic Attacks Too

Anxiety in children is sometimes misdiagnosed as attention deficit disorder or hyperactivity. Sometimes the child or adolescent is simply labeled "difficult." If you suspect anxiety disorder in your child or adolescent, I strongly suggest you work with a good child therapist who specializes in anxiety. If your child shows symptoms of anxiety and panic attacks, talk with the school counseling center and give your child books and other information to help him or her gain a better understanding of the situation.

My anxiety began when I was a child; I had my first panic attack at the age of seven. There were five kids in the family and I shared the bedroom off the kitchen with my sister Donna. We would lie in bed at night, waiting for Dad to come home.

Dad was a complex character. When he wasn't drinking, he was a delightful man. Everyone loved him and thought the world of him, but when he drank, his personality completely changed. Sometimes after a drinking binge, he would rummage around the kitchen late at night, rattling the pots and pans, making himself something to eat. He was loud and out of control. He frightened me when he'd been drinking.

One night, I was lying in bed staring at the mint green

walls, when I heard the front door open and then slam shut. Dad was home and he obviously had been drinking. He did what he usually did: he walked into the kitchen and started talking out loud to himself and making a racket. My bed was right next to the wall. I began trembling so hard, the whole bed shook. I looked up at the shadows on the wall and I saw a strange semi-human form on the wall beside me. I still don't know what it actually was reflecting, possibly a toy or a doll, but it frightened me. Then I gazed out the window and I saw hands on the clothesline. They must have been gloves that were hanging out to dry, but remember, I was only seven. Something about the shadow and the outdoors felt ominous, like a big old genie was climbing up the wall of my room and strange hands were dangling from a line out in the back yard.

Suddenly, I felt terrorizing fear. I jumped up out of bed and ran down the hallway to get my mother. I was in a panic, afraid for my life. "There's nothing out there," she assured me. "There's nothing to be afraid of." In my mind, there was a monster out there, a horrifying thing trying to get me. For nights after that, I couldn't fall asleep. I lay there, stiff as a board, certain that something was lurking just outside my window, waiting for me. That was my first panic attack, the beginning of a chain that escalated over the years.

Anxiety disorder in children can be broken down into three major types. *Separation anxiety* includes fear of getting lost and fear of germs, illnesses, and bee stings. It also covers social and performance concerns like being criticized, teased, and making mistakes. Eighty percent of children who refuse to go to school have separation anxiety.

When children experience *overanxious disorder*, they worry about future events, past behaviors, and their competence. They often complain about physical problems such as headaches and stomachaches or feelings of tension. These children are self-conscious and continually need to be reassured. These overanxious symptoms are common to the general population of children, but they predominantly affect girls.

Avoidance disorder manifests essentially in avoiding contact with unfamiliar people. The fear is often severe enough to interfere with most of the child's social relationships. Mild avoidance is quite common in children of all ages, but again, girls report more fears than boys.

Environmental stress is a prominent factor in the development of children's simple phobias. They are often linked with familial patterns. They also can be genetic. Children with parents who have anxiety disorders are seven times more likely to have their own problems with anxiety.

If you are the parent of an anxious or sensitive child, chances are, you or your spouse have suffered with anxiety. It will be difficult to help your child if you are presently suffering or in denial about your own condition. Get help. Once you recover, you can share your skills with your child. You'll feel better and you'll probably be a much better parent.

❈ **The earlier you can identify your child's anxiety, the easier it will be to treat it.**

The sooner your child learns to recognize and understand anxiety, the easier it will be to avoid panic attacks. If you think your son or daughter might be experiencing anxiety disorder, please contact a reputable child therapist in your area and talk about your concerns. At the Midwest Center, we offer a wonderfully insightful tape called The Sensitive Child for parents of anxious children.

Now let's go on to a specific example of a child's anxiety.

Anguish in a Circle

Here I am, caught up in circles.
Can't figure out why I feel I want to cry.
I see how I used to be.
Why can't I feel normal again?
I need a friend to show me the way,
To be happy.
What is happiness?
I've been so long without it.
I need to feel it,
See it,
And be it.
I need help to jump out of the circle
That defines all worry,
And makes anxiety feel worse than it is.
Help me cry.
Who will listen?
Who will care?
I need to tell someone
Who?
Who can make the pain go away
And make the world seem lighter?
I need to see,
The only one
Who can help myself is
Me.

Danielle is a gifted poet with the ability to express herself well beyond her years. She is a twelve-year-old child who wrote the above poem when she first entered the program. She contacted the Midwest Center after a long string of painful events.

When she was very young, she was fine, but as an adolescent, she began to fear going to school. Eventually, it got so bad, she became housebound. Her mother had to home-school her. She suspected what was wrong with her daughter but wasn't sure. When she finally found help from the Midwest Center, she was relieved to find that her child simply suffered from anxiety.

With terrific support from her parents, Danielle was committed to healing. Every night before she went to bed, she listened to one of the tapes from my Attacking Anxiety program. She completed the tapes about a year ago, has done extremely well since then, and she keeps on getting better. Today she can leave the house and actually enjoys it, she can be with her friends, and enthusiasm has replaced a good portion of her fear. She is truly an inspiration to us all.

THE HEALING PATH

I had been completely inundated and overwhelmed by anxiety since my childhood. What is more important than the details of my panic is the story of my power, of how I came to understand what was wrong, how I went about healing it, and how I used my personality traits to make my life rewarding and fulfilling.

What is important is to identify the problem of anxiety and panic attacks and then try to find the possible causes. If your anxiety is genetic or environmental, then you might be naturally prone to panic attacks. Sometimes it is not clear where your anxiety originated. Possibly you came from a great family environment and there's no anxiety disorder in your family. That's okay. The origin of your anxiety only serves you in the diagnosis of your condition. This information is not necessary for recovery.

❈**No matter what caused your anxiety disorder or panic attacks, the way home will be the path of acceptance, trust, and change in perception.**

My daughter Brittany and I once picked up a kitten at a pet store. We put him in a carry box to take him home, but as soon as we got into the car, he started meowing like crazy. He was terrified; he was with strange people, hearing strange sounds, all closed up in a cardboard cat box. Brittany was concerned. "Mommy, can we please take him out of the box?" she pleaded with me.

"I don't know, honey," I answered. "Cats don't do well in cars. They don't like the traffic noises."

The cat continued to cry. "Please, Mom, please can I let him out of the box?" Brittany wouldn't back down.

I decided to give it a try. I didn't like the cat crying any more than she did. She opened the box slowly and pulled out the poor, terrified kitten, placing him on her little lap. His ears were back. His spine was tense. She reached down, petting him, gently scratching his little head, and speaking in whispers. "It's okay," she cooed. "It's really okay. You'll be just fine."

The kitten looked around, evaluating his environment. I expected him to run, to hide, to leap behind the seat and dive into the first dark crevice he could find. But he didn't. He listened to Brittany's soothing voice and he felt her soft hands petting him. He began to relax, to trust us, himself, and the seemingly ominous environment. He stretched out on her lap and remained there all the way home. His environment hadn't changed; it was his perception of his environment that had changed. He no longer perceived danger, so there wasn't any.

How often do we misinterpret the condition of our surroundings and prepare ourselves for disaster? There we sit, huddled, worrying and obsessing about a non-existent danger. If only we had changed our perception and prevented the anxious feelings, we also would have prevented the panic attack. Then we could have been totally immersed in enjoying the present moment.

A Six-Part Approach to Self-Control

Panic attacks are not a laughing matter. They are painful, distressing, and exhausting, but they won't kill you. If they did, I'd be long gone. Since I had them for most of my life, I've tried everything to heal them. After years of trial and error, extensive research, and reactions from others who have tested out my methods, I've come up with a six-part approach to self-control when dealing with a panic attack. It has worked for me, for thousands of other people, and it can work for you, too.

1. Recognize that you are feeling anxious. Accept your body feelings as a symptom of your anxiety and a sign that something is bothering you. Don't let these feelings scare you.

2. Try to figure out what really is bothering you. Is it some type of conflict you don't want to deal with? Is it a scary thought? Is it a ridiculous expectation that you have on yourself? How about the television program you watched last night? Did you drink caffeine or eat chocolate? What is getting to you?

3. Give yourself permission to feel anxious about whatever is bothering you. "Of course I feel anxious because I haven't flown in a while, or I don't like confronting someone. It's okay and normal to have anxiety."

4. Use compassionate self-talk to move yourself through the anxious time. It will pass. Examples might be, "It's just anxiety. It will go away. I will not lose control. I can still go about my business feeling spaced out. It won't hurt me." This will help your system to calm down more quickly and help you get through the anxious moment more comfortably. (This is an important concept. We will be covering positive dialogue more fully in Chapter 8.)

5. Get busy. Do something to release some of this self-

induced stimulation. Your body is like a car in high gear with the brakes on. Don't just sit there. Walk. Run. Clean closets. Do something productive with the energy. This will also get your mind out of the anxiety.

6. Try to see a little humor in the way you feel. You may feel weird, but you don't look weird. No one else is noticing. Don't overreact to your symptoms. Make light of them. Laugh at yourself a little. No big deal.

Above all, be patient with yourself. It takes time and lots of compassion to rid yourself of panic attacks. But anyone can do it. Once you understand the origin and you have the skills to work through your anxiety, you will begin to minimize the attack, both in intensity and duration. Eventually you'll be able to prevent them from happening at all. Won't that be wonderful? If you put the same amount of energy toward recovery as you put toward scaring yourself, success is certain.

To overcome panic and anxiety you must face it head on and let yourself float through it, using your new skills. When you no longer allow it to frighten you, you'll see that it won't hurt you. There is no need to run. You are your safe place and your safe person. You and only you can make yourself feel better. What a powerful sense of security this will give you.

CHAPTER 4

PERSONALITY TRAITS:
VARIATIONS ON THE
ANXIOUS ATTITUDE

❦ The one thing over which you have absolute control is your own thoughts. It is this that puts you in a position to control your own destiny.

—PAUL G. THOMAS

Don't go any further. Close this book, mark your page, and on a blank piece of paper, write your personal definition of "being in control." Don't look it up, read ahead, or ask anybody else. Just write down what being in control means to you. It can be a few sentences, a paragraph, a page or several pages. Do it now, save it for later, and then come back and continue to read.

Welcome back! Was that easy or difficult? Have you ever stopped to define this concept for yourself? For me, being in control means something different in this stage of my life than when I first tried to define it. It used to mean making decisions about how I thought I should look and feel in every aspect of my life. Physically and emotionally. Being in control meant having to "appear" in control at all costs and at all times.

Fortunately, I have developed a new understanding of true control. I know that I can't predict or control what will happen all the time because life is often unpredictable. But I can decide what my reactions will be. Today, being in control means deciding how I am going to let things affect me. I can make a mental decision to feel a certain way and I can choose to respond in a less anxious, more relaxed manner. This is true control. This is what makes us feel good about ourselves. When we feel confident about our ability to control our emotions and when we are comfortable with ourselves, then and only then are we in control, because we are in control of our lives. The following sentence may be the most important one in this book.

❧ **The cause of your anxiety is the way you think.**

Our thoughts are what determine our misery and our happiness. We think ourselves into anxiety and we can think ourselves out of it. Do you want to change your life? Change the way you think. This book will show you how.

ANXIETY-PRONE PERSONALITY TRAITS

Individual personality traits can be used either positively or negatively to determine the flow of our lives. Let's begin this section with a list of the different personality traits that are common to anxiety-prone people. With a strong commitment to change your old destructive habits, with some patience, compassion, and dedicated practice, the energy behind the negative, destructive personality trait on the left can be transformed into the creative, positive energy trait on the right. I'll show you how as we progress through the chapter. We can go from:

- Perfectionism to High standards
- Inner nervousness to High vitality
- Overreactive to Healthy perspective
- Guilt feelings to Taking action
- Criticism sensitivity to Personal insight
- Emotional sensitivity to Knowing yourself
- High expectations to Realizing dreams
- Indecisiveness to Allowing mistakes
- Obsessive worrying to Goal setting
- Overidentifying to Compassion
- Fearful thoughts to Reality
- Hypochondriasis to Health
- False control to Real control

Now, let's break down these different personality traits and explore how we can transform them into something positive that will help us in controlling our anxiety and our lives. The energy is the same. How we choose to use it is up to us. Why not use it to make ourselves stronger, healthier, less anxious, and more confident?

Perfectionism to High Standards

I once received a letter from a woman I'll call Alison. She wrote: "My house has to be perfect. Everything has to be in order, everything has to look straightened and organized. I can't leave my house until it's squeaky clean and sometimes I vacuum several times a day. If things aren't clean and neat, it makes me anxious."

That's a perfectionist. Some people are perfectionistic about going to church every Sunday, others must have immaculate houses, still others wear full makeup at all times. When we speak of perfectionism, we are talking about expectations. Things aren't right until they're done your way. According to my friend Connie Szollosi, a perfectionist is someone whose favorite song is "My Way," by Frank Sinatra, someone who wants the toilet paper to come down the front of the roll. If it isn't right, you change it, even in other people's houses! I always laugh when she talks about it, but it really isn't funny because this need for things to be a certain way causes horrible anxiety.

Perfectionists have thoughts like this: "The house needs to be immaculate all the time in case a neighbor stops by; therefore, the kids shouldn't have toys in the living room and everyone has to remove his shoes, and I certainly don't want the mess of owning a dog." Does this sound like you? Does your hair have to be perfect? Does your makeup have to be on before you go to the grocery store? Do you have to find the perfect man before you can consider dating? Do your children have to behave like angels and be clean all the time so at least it "appears" they're perfect? If this sounds familiar, you're not really living. While you're wearing yourself out striving for the appearance of perfection, you may be missing out on some of life's most spontaneous, special moments.

This kind of striving gives you immense anxiety. You're not a good enough mother or a good enough wife, or daughter or employee. You're not even good enough for yourself. This "not good enough" syndrome infects every aspect of your life. You might think you're not good enough to be successful in love, in business, or even to recover from anxiety. Can you imagine the message this behavior sends out to your children?

I used to have tremendous anxiety every holiday, especially at Christmas. I would anticipate things not being perfect, so of course, they weren't. They never are. And nobody has a family like the Waltons. I used to have to go to five different Christmas tree lots before I found the perfect tree, and then it was never perfect when we got it home. That made me anxious. Christmas shopping was overwhelming because I had to find the perfect present for everyone. Even the wrapping had to be perfect. That made me anxious.

I felt I had to be the one to make sure our family had the perfect Christmas and if it wasn't perfect, I felt disappointed and guilty. I thought I had let everyone else down. That made me anxious. As a result of my expectations and the pressure I put on myself, my anticipation of Christmas nearly ruined the holiday before it began.

When I started the Midwest Center, I had a hard time letting other people do things I was committed to doing. The company was growing and there were letters to respond to, phone calls to take, people to help, lectures to give; it was overwhelming. I couldn't do it all by myself any more, so I slowly brought in wonderful, talented, dedicated people to work with me, to help me help people, to ease the pressure. Yet it was hard to let them do anything because I was afraid they might not do it my way. The funny thing is, once they got involved and developed their own style of helping people, answering the support line and writing letters, in turn, they also would have a difficult time letting someone else share that same responsibility, because that person might not do it "their way."

Many women have busy households, big families, and they work full time. Help with their cleaning would make their busy lives a lot easier, but they can't hire cleaning help. They don't think anyone can do a good enough job. Many people have employees or coworkers who could be of tremendous help to them if they would learn to ask for help, be specific about their needs and desires, and most importantly, get comfortable with giving up the "control" of doing it themselves. You need to ease up on your perfectionism and need for control and give people the opportunity to do it their way, make a few mistakes and develop their own style. They will grow and feel good about themselves as a result of your faith in them, and you will gain a sense of relief as you delegate some of the responsibility to someone else. And don't forget, the same rule applies to letting children help.

Your life could be a lot easier if you learned to delegate, to allow someone else to step in and do things for you. Although we all need help sometimes, perfectionists can't accept help, because they know that no one can do things the way they can. When I was first married, I had a hard time letting David help me clean the kitchen. I couldn't stand it if he left crumbs on the counter or if he left a wet dishrag in the sink. Once, when he did the laundry, he shrank my favorite sweater, and I wondered secretly if he had done it on purpose so he wouldn't have to do the laundry any more. Of course, he hadn't. He had just made an honest mistake. But I didn't like it! So I didn't let him do the laundry again for a long time. This was my loss, because I could have used the help.

What if you could transform the negative energy of perfectionism into the positive energy of having high standards? Having high standards is a different story, the opposite side of the perfectionist coin. While aiming for perfection can be painful and impossible, having high standards can bring us a great deal of satisfaction and joy. When we know we've done our best, we can take great comfort in a job well done. I still want things to be the best that they can be, but I'm not willing to make myself sick over it. I want a clean house, but I also want to be able to live in it. I like to do my housecleaning on Saturday, but if Saturday is a beautiful day and the sun is shining, I want to get out and enjoy it. The house will still be there when I get back. I want to be the best I can be at whatever I do professionally and give 150 percent of my effort. I want to be the best mother I can be for my children and a good wife to my husband. I do the best I can and at the end of the day I say, "Okay, I did good." Maybe it wasn't perfect, maybe it wasn't as good as yesterday, maybe it was better, but however I've done, I love myself as I am, unconditionally.

One of the most wonderful gifts I can offer my children is to help them believe that they don't have to be perfect. As a matter of fact, although I have taught them to have high standards, I have also taught them not to strive for perfection because it doesn't exist. It's similar to the misconception that things should always be fair. Often, they just aren't. It's the same with perfection. Nothing and no one is perfect. So, if there's no such thing as perfection, how do we know when we've done our best? That's easy. When we can say to ourselves, "I feel good about what I just did," or "I'm proud of that," or "I feel good about myself for making that effort." How about, "It didn't work out but I gave it a heck of a try." When we can say any of these things, then we've accomplished something!

❦ **Instead of striving for perfection, strive to get comfortable with the fact that things aren't perfect and never will be.**

With perfectionism, you are never satisfied. With high standards, you feel proud of yourself and the work that you do. The bottom line is that being perfect is impossible. When you pretend to be perfect, it makes you feel as if you're lying inside. Releasing your perfectionism is a setup for freedom from anxiety.

You don't have to compromise your standards when you release perfectionism. You can still do your best and feel good while you're doing it. Having high standards leads to a more confident you, pride in yourself, pride in the people in your life, and knowing that whatever you do is the best that it can be.

Inner Nervousness to High Vitality

There is an energy we create with our thoughts that makes us feel electrified. As discussed earlier, this energy results from the release of adrenaline. If we don't know what to do with it, it can scare us half to death as it surges through our bodies. It makes us feel nervous, as if we're jumping out of our skins and we can't control it. Remember: we created the energy ourselves. Used properly, this change can be a great source of power.

This energy can empower you, make you more productive, and assist you in doing wonderful things. If we turn the energy inward where it can be of no use, the result is fear and anxiety. The energy turned outward, where it belongs, can empower us. Athletes thrive on adrenaline. They have loads of energy that they deliberately create with their minds. They rev themselves up for action; they run, they sprint, they dart and dive. They eat foods that create energy.

Each time I get up to do a lecture or a seminar, sometimes in front of thousands of people, I have this same energy. I need it to do my work effectively because if I didn't have access to this high energy, I wouldn't be an exciting speaker. If I didn't know how to use the energy, I might be anxious and afraid. I might choose not to speak at all, not wanting to feel this anticipatory energy. What's important is to recognize this feeling, label it "vitality," and use it accordingly. Clean closets, exercise, go dancing, or do whatever else you enjoy. You could write or draw; you could cook something wonderful for dinner. The possibilities are endless.

If you can turn this energy around and use it creatively, you will be able to accomplish great things. You'll be able to stand in front of a group of people and give a fabulous presentation. You'll be able to step up your exercise program. You'll be able to write a beautiful story, organize your house, or get outside and play with your children.

❀**How you interpret the energy—as negative inner nervousness or positive creative vitality—is all up to you.**

I once went on a skiing trip, my second time on the slopes. There was a woman in my beginner's class whom I'll never forget. She had a big laugh that filled the room, and she gave off a positive glow that everybody loved. She was also quite a big woman. I remember riding up in the ski lift with her just in front of me. I was fearfully anticipating skiing down the hill fast, and I thought to myself, "I wonder how she feels on skis? Is she apprehensive because of her weight?"

We got off the lift, she was still in front of me, and as we took off down the slope, I heard her yell, "Yaaaa hoooo!" She shouted with joy the whole way down; she was having the time of her life. I wasn't. I was in terror, and instead of yelling with joy, I was silently reciting my mantra, "I'm going to get hurt! I'm going to die!" We ended up at the bottom of the hill a few minutes apart, both standing on our feet, but she was elated and I was panicked. I knew I needed to speak with this woman.

I made my way over to her and said, "Can we ride back up together?"

"Sure!" she answered, practically running to get to the lift.

As we sat side by side in the chair, ascending the mountain, I asked her, "Why is it when you go down that hill, you're obviously having a ball? And I'm right behind you, scared out of my wits. My heart is pounding, my hands are sweating, and I can't breathe."

She looked at me, her face flushed with anticipation, and laughed her booming laugh. "I feel the exact same way you do. My heart is pounding, my hands are sweating, and I can hardly breathe. But you're seeing it as fear and I'm seeing it as excitement. If you told yourself you were excited, you'd have a whole different feeling about the trip down."

I could hardly believe what she was saying. It was like a light bulb going off in my head. She was right. I could change my thoughts, change my mind, and change my experience. We got off the lift and I started down, but this time my self-talk was different. "All right," I told myself. "My heart's beating hard and my palms are sweaty. I'm totally excited! These feelings aren't gonna kill me. I'm not gonna die. It's okay for my heart to pound, for my palms to sweat. It's okay to anticipate. I'm excited!"

I flew down that hill and when I got to the bottom, I was hooked. I had fallen in love with skiing and I'm a ski enthusiast to this day. I'll never forget that large woman flying down the hill in front of me as if she were as light as air. In that moment, she was! It's all in the mind.

Overreactive to Healthy Perspective

When you are in an agitated state, you are all worked up. Someone touches you and you jump. The phone rings and you're startled. A sudden loud noise shocks you. Anxious people overreact to anything from bad news, to a sad television show, to a turbulent flight. We take everything personally and literally; we take everything to extremes.

In the past, I was too afraid to go into business for myself. I knew that with business came the possibility of things like disagreements or even lawsuits. The thought of such confrontations was overwhelming; I felt incapable of standing up to any of it. This is common for people with anxiety. We hate conflict, which we avoid like the plague because we overreact to negative or difficult situations. We might get hysterical or, at the very least, upset. We immediately begin obsessing about what could happen next. With anxiety, one thing leads to the next thing and before we know it, we're back on the treadmill. Since the experience is so painful, we avoid it if we can. Unfortunately, we also end up avoiding many wonderful opportunities.

❅**When we learn to put things in proper perspective, we are in control and we no longer have to be afraid. We can be positive instead of negative, rational instead of irrational.**

I used to hate to fly. When there was turbulence, the negative thoughts would come and I'd start obsessing, "what-ifing," and convincing myself that I was about to die. "What if we hit an air pocket, what if we crash, what if the plane goes down?" That's overreacting. One of the worst flight experiences I ever had was from Detroit to Los Angeles. For the first few hours, the ride was smooth and I could see the ground from my window seat. I was relaxed, reading a magazine, when out of the blue the pilot's voice filled the cabin.

"Hello, ladies and gentlemen. This is Captain Martin. We are approaching the Colorado Rockies. During this time of the year, there is often substantial turbulence in this area as a result of changing wind patterns. We ask that you fasten your seat belts and remain seated. Also, we ask that the flight attendants please be seated."

By the time I had fastened my seat belt, my heart was pounding and my hands were sweating. I gripped the arms of my seat and prepared for the worst. Then the pilot added, "We'll be approaching this area in approximately seventeen minutes." That was the longest seventeen minutes of my life! My eyes were riveted on my watch while my legs shook, my heart pounded, my sweaty hands clutched, and my breathing got heavier by the minute. While I waited, I darted my gaze around. Other people were drinking, taking pills, and attempting to distract themselves.

"How could he do that to us?" I thought to myself. "How bad is it going to be? He must expect it to be pretty bad if he made the flight attendants sit down! How long will it last? What if I get sick? What if it's really bad? Why did I take this flight?" As my mind raced with anticipation, I monitored the lapsed time. Ten minutes, fifteen minutes, twenty-two minutes. I was exhausted from worry. "How will I get through this?" I moaned to myself. "I'm already totally stressed out, and we haven't even hit the turbulence yet." Suddenly, the seat belt signs went off. The flight attendants were up now, serving drinks and chatting. I spoke to one of them. "Excuse me," I said. "When are we going to hit that turbulent area?"

He looked at me with a shrug of his shoulder. "We passed over it several minutes ago. There wasn't any turbulence. What would you like to drink?"

"WHAT!" I thought to myself. "I JUST MADE MYSELF SICK AND I'M A TOTAL NERVOUS WRECK...FOR NOTHING!" I sat there in total disbelief about what I had just done to myself.

I had anticipated something happening and I made myself sick or anxious when there was no danger or real problem. We have a choice to make about the messages we give ourselves. Since we choose to be anxious, we also can choose not to be anxious. We can choose to react differently. We can say to ourselves, "What's real here? What is the likelihood that my worst fear will actually happen?"

Usually slim to not at all. For example, turbulence means nothing more than bumpy air. It's a normal experience in flying and airplanes are prepared for it. They are built to handle it. It doesn't mean danger or death. Did you know that you are more likely to die from a bee sting than an airplane crash? Did you know that your chance of being struck dead by lightning is 1 in 1.9 million and your chance of dying in an airplane crash is 1 in 10 million? You're much more likely to die on a bicycle, in a car, or in a natural disaster than on a commercial airline flight. If you get information and become educated about your fears, you'll be rational and able to put things in perspective.

When our first impulse is to panic and to obsess, how do we accomplish the task of putting things in proper perspective? We need to take control of our minds, so we start by stopping. Clear your mind. Start being rational. When you hear yourself beginning to obsess, just say, "Time out!" Then stop, breathe deeply, and say to yourself, "I absolutely want to change. I want to stop the vicious cycle I'm creating. I'm going to start working on it now. I need to go in a different direction and be loving and supportive to myself. How can I use this energy positively? What does this really mean to me? Am I really in danger or am I just overreacting? Am I feeling insecure, and if so, why? What can I do to make myself feel more secure?" It takes practice and training, but the rewards are well worth the effort.

It's never too late to take control of your mind. If you've already triggered the chemical response, you can still turn it around. Even when the adrenaline has been released, that's when you pull out a pen and paper and write. At home, instead of worrying about your job, do something physical that's fun or productive. On the airplane when you're anticipating turbulence, when you're feeling that all too familiar rush of energy, talk to someone. Get into the moment and be where you are. All of these actions will take your mind off yourself and allow it to release some of the negative thoughts. Then, you can ease up, put things into the right perspective, and stop your anxiety from ruining your moment, and potentially, your life.

Guilt Feelings to Taking Action

Guilt is often associated with low self-esteem, with feelings of inferiority, lack of confidence, thinking we're not good enough, or that we did something unforgivable. We tend to view ourselves in unloving ways and beat ourselves up, certain that we could have been better, that we should have been smarter or more sensitive or that we should have known better. We give ourselves grief, judging ourselves, certain that others are doing the same. What a draining way to go through life! How useless to be so hard on ourselves about something that happened in the past which we have no possibility of changing. If we feel guilty about something that's happening now, we can use our guilt as motivation to change it.

❧**There's another way of working with the energy we produce when we feel guilty about something we did. We can use it to recognize our mistakes and to motivate change.**

Perhaps you need to apologize to someone. Perhaps you need to write a letter or to figure out a new way of behaving. Instead of getting down on yourself, telling yourself how horrible you are, treat yourself with compassion. You deserve it. Life is a learning process; it's natural and human to make mistakes. Recognize your guilt, redirect your thoughts and improve yourself. If you're condemning yourself or beating yourself up, you're disempowering yourself. When your vital forces are drained, you can't do anything to change because you have no energy. Treat yourself with kindness by saying, "I'm not a bad person. I simply did something that was wrong. I'll learn from my mistakes and I won't do it again. I'm human."

You're not a bad mother because you have a full-time job. Use this as a message, not a baseball bat! Maybe you need to spend more time with your kids. You're not a bad husband because you work so much. Maybe you need to reassess your priorities, tell your wife you feel guilty and then start delegating more. When you use your guilt feelings as a messenger, whatever you did has value because you learned from it. You've stopped blaming yourself and started taking positive action. You're not a bad person; you simply made a mistake. Join the human race. Once you've evaluated your actions without blame, you can take positive action that will alleviate the guilt.

Criticism Sensitivity to Personal Insight

People who are prone to anxiety are prone to being sensitive. We take criticism personally. We get our feelings hurt and then we put up our guard. Nobody likes to hear negative things said about them, but sometimes it happens, and sometimes it's even good for us. We can't go through life avoiding criticism because if we tried, we'd have to avoid people. Criticism is a natural part of life because everybody has different opinions and different ways of doing things. Unfortunately, few have perfected the fine art of criticizing with love. It sometimes comes out unskillfully, sounding like negative input, even when it isn't meant that way. Somebody's feelings may get hurt, although this was not the original intention. If you are the object of someone's criticism, even if he is not tactful or is even hostile, you can look at it in a different way and learn from it.

❇The truth is, criticism can be good for you. Use it to
  grow.

When someone has given you a criticism, in either a loving
or a hostile way, this is a signal to take a ten-second time
out. Ask yourself, "What can I learn from this? What
insight does this person have, no matter what her style of
delivery may be? Can I use her ideas to discover something new? Is what she is saying something that can ultimately create a better me?" Whether it's said with flowers
or angry words, you probably can use criticism to learn
and gain insight about yourself, especially if you're honest
with yourself. This can be very freeing. Instead of the initial reaction of defensiveness, you are now stepping back
and taking a ten-second time out to evaluate. You're out of
the line of fire, outside the situation looking in. You're less
involved emotionally. You are simply there to observe and
learn.

Emotional Sensitivity to Knowing Yourself

Emotionally sensitive people usually cry easily. Little
things bother them. Typically, anxious people are very sensitive: to criticism, to scary movies, to sad events, to fearful
situations, to medications and different types of food. This
kind of person tends to overreact and overidentify. When I
was severely agoraphobic, if I read a newspaper article
about someone hurting another person, or doing something that I considered out of control, I was afraid that I
might do it, too. If I felt strange and spacey, was I susceptible to doing something out of control? But it was only fear.
I knew inside that I would never really do any of those
things.

❋The sensitivity that makes you vulnerable also can give you the ability to know yourself well, to excel and do great things.

I've learned to see my sensitivity as a gift, but I have to be aware of how sensitive I really am. I listen to myself and I know what works for me and what doesn't. I understand that stimulants such as chocolate or caffeine might make me irritable or edgy. I know that there are certain medications I don't tolerate well. My sensitive nature is an asset to my career; I utilize it to be compassionate to other people's pain and needs. It helps me with my mothering, and my children are gentle as a result of my being that way with them. As a result of living with me, my husband also has gained a new understanding of being sensitive to someone else.

Use your sensitivity to your advantage. Discern which people will enhance your life and which will drain you. Know what television shows you can watch and which ones you can't. Years ago, shortly after I had recovered, a group of friends were going to see a movie about a psychotic serial killer and I chose not to join them. I knew that I shouldn't watch sick horror movies; I was too sensitive and I never liked them anyway. Before I had my recovery skills, I probably would have gone and then obsessed over it, but I was able to save myself the suffering.

Learn which medications you can handle and which you can't. People who need antidepressants must take side-effects into consideration if they are particularly sensitive to such things. We will discuss this more fully in Chapter 13, but for now, suffice it to say that if you and your doctor know your sensitivities, you can make intelligent decisions about whether or not to move forward with certain medications. If you are affected strongly by a medicine that someone else can easily tolerate, it doesn't make you bad or wrong. It simply means that your body works differently.

It's great to be a sensitive person; sensitive people make the best lovers, the best parents, and the best friends, the best employers, the best employees, the best actors, the best writers, the best doctors, the best poets. Now don't you feel special? That's what I've been trying to tell you. You are!

High Expectations to Realizing Dreams

Setting unrealistic goals is similar to being a perfectionist. You're someone who either sets goals that are impossible to reach, or you demand a level of performance that neither you nor anyone else can live up to. You expect things from other people that they can't do, and so you're being constantly let down. You set goals too high for yourself, so you're always failing. Nothing and nobody is ever good enough. You live in a constant state of disappointment.

High expectations by themselves are not the problem. It's okay to have goals and it's okay for them to be fabulous. In my seminars, I always tell people to shoot for the stars, to go for the top. But it's okay if you don't make it. We have to learn to accept ourselves whether we win or lose. Take risks, go after your dreams. If you remove the focus from the results and enjoy the trip, you'll keep it all in perspective. Nothing ever lives up to your complete expectations. That's the way life is. It helps to understand that:

❄**Happiness doesn't come "some day when." It comes from inside yourself, right now, wherever you are.**

We've all heard the story about the young woman who waited for happiness. She was caught up in the "I'll be happy when" trap. "I'll be happy when I get into college. I'll be happy when I get out of college. I'll be happy when I get married. I'll be happy when I have children, when I get some time alone, when I can quit my job, when I get back to work. I'll be happy when, when, when..." This person finds herself asking "When *will* I be happy? How about now? This is not a dress rehearsal; this is it!" Let yourself be happy with the smallest of things.

A wealthy, professionally successful man who went through the Attacking Anxiety program once told me how much he envied me.

"Why?" I asked him, amazed that the man who appeared to have everything might envy me.

"You obviously love what you do and do what you love," he answered. "I can see it in your eyes, hear it in the sound of your voice. I worked hard all my life struggling and pushing myself, doing something I didn't really enjoy because I thought I'd be so successful, I'd finally be happy and enjoy my life. Well, it took most of my life to get here and I wish I'd have enjoyed the trip more."

"What would you have done differently?" I asked him.

"I would have done something I loved. Something that felt good." We better have good memories of the climb, because in the end, maybe that's all we'll have.

What makes for happiness varies from person to person. What is realistic for one may be unrealistic for another. If you don't know the difference, talk to contented people. See what their criterion is for happiness. If your expectations are giving you anxiety instead of providing motivation, if you're attached to the outcome, your expectations are probably unrealistic. If you're not attached to the outcome, then you'll be okay, whatever your dreams are. If you don't get the house on the hill or the Mercedes or the perfect relationship, would you view your life as useless? Would you see yourself as unsuccessful? I hope not. Those things are nice goals but they won't keep you happy. Find some goals that will bring you peace. How about a goal to get more enjoyment from your present moments? Do you appreciate your health and the fact that you can get up each day and walk out into the sunshine? Maybe a goal to look more closely at the people in your inner circle and the uniqueness they offer. How about allowing yourself to enjoy more physical touch or warm conversations, or play-time with friends or your children.

If your expectations for your happiness are dependent upon someone else, that's another sign that you're being unrealistic. All you can ever receive from another is more insight about yourself. You are the only one who can give you what you want: permission to be happy. When we drop unrealistic expectations, we can begin to look within to find the inspiration and the motivation to follow our dreams and to find true happiness.

Indecisiveness to Allowing Mistakes

Do you have a hard time making decisions? If you do, you probably have a lack of confidence in yourself and in your ability to take risks, stay committed, and follow through. If you have trouble making decisions, you are most likely afraid of making mistakes and failing. You probably have a difficult time making a decision because of your subconscious fear that you will make the wrong one and create an immense amount of anxiety.

We tend to think that everything is written in stone, that decisions and minds can't be changed. It isn't and they can. No decision is perfect.

❄**There are no right or wrong decisions. You simply need to make one and accompany it with a commitment to do your best to make it work.**

Once again, it's about putting things in perspective. Perhaps you think your whole life is riding on one decision. If this sounds like your way of thinking, you're probably overreacting. Get a better perspective on what part this decision really is playing in your life. Get as much information as you can and then make your decision based upon that information. You can't be certain which decision will serve you best. You can only choose one, try it, and commit yourself to it 100 percent. If it doesn't work, let it go and make another one.

Ambivalence is painful. Use it as motivation to investigate your situation. Your anxiety is a signal that a decision needs to be made. It's time to educate yourself about the decision, become more informed about the various directions available, pick one road, follow it, and do your best. The final outcome isn't nearly as important as the confidence you gain by becoming a clear decision-maker. Very often, the final outcome changes along the way. What matters is that when it's time to decide, movement in any direction will release your anxiety and give you a sense of taking control.

Obsessive Worrying to Goal-Setting

We are very creative people. Unfortunately for us, our creativity often leads to obsessive, worrisome thoughts. This means that we get one thought in our minds and we dwell on it, repeating it over and over again. We tend to be overly analytical; we need answers and we need them now. We want the whys and the hows. We want the details. We want to know how long it will last, where it will end up, and why it has to be this way. Then we begin to visualize the worst possible scenario and before you know it, we are a walking chemical factory, riddled with adrenaline and anxiety, amazed that we ended up this way once again.

❀Instead of obsessing about something negative, we can use our analytical obsessive energy to visualize and create something wonderful.

To get in touch with your obsessive thinking patterns, answer the following questions as honestly as possible:

What is your most common obsessive thought?
How often do you obsess about this? When does it seem to come on? When you're tired? Before bed? Any other time?
Can you pinpoint what you don't want to deal with that is causing you to think obsessive thoughts?
What could you do to face this problem?

Now write a paragraph about your obsessive thought. Don't worry how bad it may look or if it makes you anxious to write it.

What if I go crazy? Could I end up in a mental institution? I couldn't live in a mental institution. Is this the beginning of insanity? Am I going to just flip out and never come back? What would happen to my kids and my family? Would anyone still love me?

Now turn the paragraph into something humorous.

I'm going to imagine myself going bananas. I'm going to picture myself in a monkey suit running up and down the street kissing people and passing out bananas.

If your obsessive thought is suicide, you might imagine yourself trying to kill yourself on an overdose of jelly-beans.
Read your answers ten times a day for the next two

weeks until it bores you. This is important. The idea here is to expose yourself to this thought enough times that it becomes old and no longer produces anxiety.

Use your obsessive energy to think about what you want in your life. How would you like to see yourself? What kind of person do you want to be and what do you want to do with your time? What do you want to change about your career and when do you want to change it? Once you have the answers, replace your negative, obsessive thoughts with positive focused ones. Be clear, strong, and defined about your positive visualization. Set a time line for yourself.

You can use the analytical thought process ruminating in your mind to get what you want. When you're obsessing about what isn't even real—which is typically what we obsess about—STOP! Take a ten-second time out. Then replace the object of your ruminations with a goal-setting procedure. Instead of focusing on something scary, focus on something you want or want to become. Use your powerful focus to bring it into your life, to write down what you want, and to set time lines on when you'll get it. Replace your obsessive anxiety with strategies to make things happen, to become the person you truly want to be. Take it from me, it works!

Overidentifying to Compassion

Have you ever listened to someone else's troubles and thought, "What if I end up with that problem?" People with anxiety and depression, when placed in group situations, tend to worry that they will take on the problems of people around them. Once again, it's a question of extreme sensitivity. We feel everything. Therapy groups that are focused on anxiety and depression can be powerful and effective, but when anxious people are put in groups with people who have various other problems, they might end up taking other people's symptoms home with them and wondering, "Am I going to get that way?"

I remember a lady in group who saw someone on the news who had hurt her children. She came to group saying, "What if I do that? I mean I don't think I would, but what if I hurt my kids?" If your sister-in-law calls you one night to talk about a friend who's suffering with cancer, you might start waking up in the middle of the night with symptoms, worrying that you have cancer.

Conversely, we still want to listen to our friends' problems and concerns. We don't want to use our suggestibility as an excuse to be uninvolved and nonsupportive, but we also don't have to take on anybody else's pain. We can understand other people's pain, be compassionate and be there for them, but we don't have to suffer along with them. Obsessing about something that doesn't belong to you exhausts the positive energy that you might give back to someone who really needs it. We can look at him and say, "Look what he has been through. What can I say to help him?" We can allow their experiences to make us more appreciative of our own lives.

❀Instead of letting other people's pain threaten you, take a step back, gain a right perspective, and be grateful for your own life.

You can say to yourself, "This is what they are going through. I don't need to identify. What can I do to help? How can I serve? How can I use what I've learned through my own experience or by reading this book to help and be there for them?" And then, be there. When you're finally home alone with yourself, instead of worrying about what might happen to you, turn the situation around. Be appreciative that it isn't you. Be grateful for the life you have and the health you have and the relationships you have, and that you can put your thoughts into perspective and control them.

Fearful Thoughts to Reality

People with anxiety disorder often have upsetting fearful thoughts. Thoughts they wouldn't admit to their closest friends for fear that they would be locked up. These thoughts run the spectrum from the fear of losing your mind, to worrying that you're going to hurt someone, to worrying that you're dying or that you might even commit suicide.

For many years, I had a fear of knives that was so terrifying, I never told anyone, not even my therapist. I, like many people who have a problem with fearful thoughts, knew that I wouldn't really hurt anyone, but I was afraid anyway. Now I understand that my fears were unfounded. At the time, they seemed very real and very frightening.

The truth of the matter is that scary thoughts about knives or anything else are only a diversion, a way of distracting ourselves from something that we need to deal with but, as yet, are unwilling to face.

The person with anxiety disorder doesn't act on scary thoughts. Those who do are people with severe mental disorders who actually find these kinds of thoughts appealing. We don't find them appealing at all. In fact, they frighten us. We think to ourselves, "Oh, my gosh, why am I thinking this? There must be something wrong with me. I'm afraid that I'm even having these thoughts at all."

If we pay attention to our minds, we can actually utilize our thought processes to wake up to the truth. We can recognize that we are allowing our minds to distract us from something we really need to take a look at or deal with. We can ask ourselves, "What's going on in my life right now that I don't want to see? Why am I choosing to scare myself and worry about hurting someone or worry that I'm getting sick, rather than dealing with what really is going on?"

The answer may be that we'd rather put ourselves through fear and anxiety than confront a potentially uncomfortable situation. One of the men in my group, Arty, had to drive over a bridge that was half a mile long to get to the weekly session. When you drive onto the bridge, there's a sign that says: DO NOT STOP ON BRIDGE! They must make bridges like this with signs like that just to test people like us! By the time you can read the sign, it's too late to go back and there's nowhere to turn around. The bridge crosses a beautiful lake and, to the average person, it's no big deal. It's a pleasant ride. People who need to be in control will immediately see that they can't get off, that they must keep going, and that they can't control their comings and goings. It's a situation custom made for agoraphobics!

When Arty finally arrived at the Midwest Center, he'd say, "I don't know what's wrong with me, but the day before I leave to come for group, I start having these horrifying thoughts of hurting myself. Then, every time I get on that bridge, I start thinking about hurting my children. I adore my children, I know I'd never hurt them. So why do I have these thoughts?" It was obvious. He was so afraid of being out of control on the bridge, he distracted himself with the most terrible thoughts he could dream up: hurting his children. It worked. The thoughts were so horrifying they effectively took his mind off the real problem: being on a bridge with no way out.

You may be in a bad relationship or a boring job or you may have low self-esteem. Rather than dealing with these issues, which would create an immense amount of anxiety, you choose to worry about losing your mind or dying or you have other scary thoughts that are completely unrealistic. They are so terrible, they absorb all of your attention and distract you. Then you can't think about getting out of that bad relationship, or changing your career, or losing that extra thirty or forty pounds. Mission accomplished; you are too obsessed to take action.

❀ **Your decision to stop your scary thoughts will allow you to pay attention to your mind and give yourself insight about something real that is bothering you.**

When you are overwhelmed with scary thoughts, don't give them any value. Instead, ask yourself, "What's wrong? Is it my relationship? Am I unhappy? How about my children? What's so difficult for me to deal with that I'm turning it inward and scaring myself?" Would you rather deal with a distraction that keeps escalating your pain or the truth that can be healed? If you pay attention to your mind, you can replace your scary thoughts with positive dialogue. I like to call this compassionate self-talk. We'll get into this more in Chapter 8. For now, practice with the following self-talk list. Then you can make up your own list to custom fit your particular thoughts.

- Anxiety is a normal emotion that I can control. I don't need to be afraid of my feelings. I will relax, distract myself, and let these feelings pass.
- I like myself. I am working to improve myself, to be stronger. I accept myself for who I am today. I will feel even stronger tomorrow and even stronger in six months.
- There are a lot of good things about me. I am talented. I am loving. I am confident.
- I am positive. I radiate good, positive feelings. I am full of life. I love life. I am very glad to be alive.

- I am intelligent. I am interested in new things and ready for new challenges.
- I have a lot of energy. I am exciting and I enjoy my own company. People enjoy being around me.
- I am sincere and honest. I am a real person. I feel good about my weaknesses and strengths. I accept myself for who I am. I am working toward being even better.
- I enjoy feelings of excitement. I want to feel life. I enjoy feeling alive.
- I deserve to be happy, to feel content. I have a right to go after the things I want in life. I will achieve them.
- I am hard-working, enthusiastic, and energetic. I am special.
- I am a good problem-solver. I am confident in my ability to make decisions. There is no problem that I can't conquer. My strength is greater than any problem I might be faced with. Problems are just opportunities to grow.
- Lines, traffic, crowds, and waits don't bother me. I don't mind spending time being patient. There is really no emergency.
- I can accomplish anything I want. Nothing stands in my way. I am strong. I am in control of my life.
- I feel calm. I have peace of mind. It is good to let my mind clear, to let thoughts drift in and out. I feel relaxed. I feel soothed.

Hypochondriasis to Health

Have you ever gone through a serious sickness or the death of a loved one, and then worried that you might die, too? Most of us have. If several family members have died of cancer, it's easy to obsess that you might end up with cancer, too. Again, hypochondriasis is a form of distraction. If you can find out what you're distracting yourself from, you're on the road to relieving yourself from much unnecessary anxiety.

❧ **If you find yourself worrying about your health, use it as motivation. Stop worrying, listen to the signals, and do something positive for yourself.**

For starters, become more health conscious. If you're worried about your heart, there are many things you can do. You can stop smoking, start exercising, and, if you're overweight, you can begin a weight loss program.

The body is a finely tuned instrument. If it's trying to tell you something, listen to it. When you begin to have anxiety, it sends you a clear message. Instead of reacting with fear, instead of fretting about what might happen, you can say to yourself, "My heart is pounding right now. I am obviously upset about something. What's going on? Maybe some exercise or a better diet will help. Do I need to decrease my alcohol or caffeine intake? Maybe I need to take better care of myself."

I remember a man named Erik who came into our office worrying that he was going to die of cancer or a heart attack, both of which ran in his family. I was amazed that he was overweight and he smoked. He said he had tried to lose weight and quit smoking, but for some reason he just couldn't do either. I wondered if his fear of an early death was an excuse for procrastination, not going after his dreams and not improving his life. Why should he end his bad marriage when he wasn't long for this world anyway? Why should he leave the job he disliked when he probably wouldn't live very long? What's wrong with this picture? Secretly the fear of ending his marriage and changing his career terrorized him. So his smoking and his weight gave him the thought distraction he needed to resist change, which he subconsciously perceived as more anxiety-producing than fear of death. Staying where we are often can be the most difficult or harmful decision.

Many people who suffer with hypochondriasis just need some attention. Give yourself permission to ask for what you need. As children, many of us got our needs met when we were ill. That was when our mothers took care of us, were sweet to us, made us our favorite foods, and let us watch our favorite shows on television. So we equated being sick with receiving attention and love.

Now that we're grown, we don't have to be sick to ask for what we want. If you whine, nobody will want to be around you, anyway. There are positive ways of getting attention from others, like asking for it. If you want to be held more, tell your partner. If you want to be heard, pick your time to speak when somebody has time and attention to listen. If you're alone, you can learn how to give that attention to yourself. Take a walk or a warm bath. Get a massage. Cuddle up with a good book or make yourself a wonderful meal. Whatever makes you feel happy and secure, give it to yourself. You deserve it.

False Control to Real Control

People with anxiety value control almost as much as they value their lives. That may sound dramatic, but it's true. If we aren't in control, we better look as if we are.

When I was in my early twenties, I hung out with a group of friends who don't remember my ever exhibiting any signs of insecurity or anxiety. I was the epitome of control. Or at least, I appeared that way. People with anxiety keep their feelings of loss of control a big secret. We think we have to. As long as no one knows how we feel, we won't risk embarrassment, which is for some, a fate worse than death.

❦When you're being real and vulnerable, intimacy comes naturally. You are confident enough to show all sides of yourself. That's the definition of real control.

Today, I let myself go. I act goofy and show my vulnerability. When I feel out of control, I don't care who sees me and what people think. The irony is that I'm more in control of my life now than when I was pretending to be. I certainly have a lot more fun. I'm relaxed and I'm myself. Appearances have become less important. I'd rather feel good than look good.

Needing to look a certain way prevents you from forming intimate relationships because in order to do so, you must reveal who you really are. Unconditional love, perhaps the greatest gift in all the world, cannot exist unless someone truly knows you. All of you. When you're trying to control the way you look, the way you act, and the way you feel, intimacy is impossible.

❦There is an appropriate time to draw on your ability to be in control, an ability that anxiety-prone people have mastered.

It takes courage and control to march out there and give a presentation to hundreds or even thousands of people when you're feeling scared, insecure, or vulnerable. You can't always be sure of how you're going to feel on any given day. Maybe you didn't sleep so well last night. Maybe you had a misunderstanding with your mate or found out that a family member was sick right before the lecture was scheduled to begin. But you can't stop the show. Things happen when they happen. These are times when your ability to be in control is appropriate. Possibly you are in a power meeting with some heavy-hitters and you're nervous. You know what they say, "Never let them see you sweat." Use your control skills to show them how confident you are!

People with anxiety are very strong. If there were a fire in a movie theater, the anxious person would be the first one to run into that closed space and rescue his child. That's because people with anxiety disorder have built such powerful muscles to appear strong and in control, we can use that same strength to give us courage. In a pinch, we'll definitely come through. After all, our whole life has felt like a pinch. Even when we learn to be vulnerable and relaxed, our automatic responses will serve us when we need them. I guarantee it. So use your control when you need it. But when you need to let the walls down, let the walls down. Finding the balance is what constitutes a healthy life. Control may be just what you need in a meeting, but at the same time, it could be a major source of pain in your personal relationships.

A gentleman named Derek was in one of my groups. He was proper, in his late fifties, very attractive, and the CEO of four major companies. Very much in control. When I first met him, I was taken aback by how powerful he appeared, yet Derek couldn't go through car washes. He had a difficult time flying and he couldn't ride in the back seat of a car. Of course, nobody knew. Everyone saw Derek as this powerful CEO and that was what he was. But it wasn't all that he was. He maintained the illusion of his invulnerability by avoiding situations that were potential embarrassments. Was Derek ever embarrassed? Never. Did he worry about embarrassing himself? You bet!

Every week, he showed up for group in a suit and tie. He looked impeccable; he sat straight and tall in his seat. Perfect posture. He never even loosened his tie. When he arrived for the fifth session, I said to him, "You know, Derek, I'd love to see you in jeans and a T-shirt." A few weeks later, Derek walked in wearing a baggy sweater and a pair of jeans. He sat down, let his back sink into the chair and beamed. We couldn't take our eyes off of him, he looked so relaxed and playful. That was the beginning of a big change in Derek's life, and it was infectious. The shift in his demeanor allowed the rest of us to feel much more comfortable around him.

Are you someone who always has to be the life of the party? When you give the party, do you have to be the perfect host? Are you always dressed perfectly, is your house immaculate, are your children's clothes pressed and clean at all times? If the answer is "yes," give yourself a break. Let yourself go, loosen up. There are places in your life where being in control is exactly what you need, like in a professional situation or a crisis. But there are times when kicking up your heels and being less controlled is far more appropriate and more fun.

Before we close this chapter, take out the piece of paper on which you wrote your definition of "being in control." Don't reread it yet. Just mark your place, close the book, write a new definition, and come back when you're finished.

Now compare the two. How have your ideas about control changed? Can you see that once you recognize the inner workings of your particular personality, the whole idea of control shifts? As we said at the beginning of the chapter:

❈ **The cause of your anxiety is the way you think.**

If you choose to use the energy behind your individual personality traits in positive pursuit of recovery, the rewards will go beyond your wildest dreams. You'll feel more relaxed, more successful and happy to be you. You'll feel in control for the first time, because you'll truly *be* in control. You'll be controlling your reactions and the effect things have on you, both in the present moment and long term. It's a wonderful feeling and that will become addictive. Your body and mind don't know the difference between a good addiction and a bad addiction. It's just as easy to get addicted to good behaviors, ones that will eventually replace your anxiety-causing behaviors. Let's get addicted to the good stuff!

CHAPTER 5

ANTICIPATORY ANXIETY:
THE "WHAT-IF" SYNDROME

❧ *Ultimately we know deeply that the other side of every fear is a freedom.*

—MARILYN FERGUSON

Dear Lucinda,

My husband has been wanting to rent a mobile home and take a trip to Canada for two years. I have wanted to go very badly but I always seem to chicken out when it comes to making the final plans. Up until recently I haven't been able to leave town comfortably, let alone leave the country!

Anyway, we decided to take the trip and we rented the camper. I was so anxious BEFORE we left I nearly didn't go. All the "what-ifs" started. "What if I get sick? What if I lose my mind hundreds of miles from home? What if I have to come back?" Despite my fears, I went.

We had a wonderful time! I was anxious and had some symptoms when we first left and at various times while we were on the trip, but the worst anxiety I had was right before we left for the trip when I was "what-ifing" and thinking about all the things that could happen.

I am so glad I didn't let my fears stop me. This trip has given me a whole new feeling of confidence and best of all we had a great time!

Grace

Here's a new twist on "what-if" thinking.

What if you overcame your panic attacks?
What if you got your self-confidence back?
What if you got that job you always wanted?
What if you could take care of yourself?
What if you could get off your medication for good?
What if you stopped feeling spacey and anxious?
What if you enjoyed driving?
What if you could travel out of the country by yourself?
What if you actually enjoyed that airplane flight?
What if you stopped worrying about your health?
What if you recovered completely?

I could go on and on, just as we do with the negative lists of what-ifs. Although we are much more accustomed to that list, the positive and negative what-ifs are both examples of anticipatory thoughts. One produces excitement and the other produces anxiety. You can make your own choice.

ANTICIPATORY ANXIETY

Anticipation is defined in Webster's Ninth *New Collegiate Dictionary* as: "the act of looking forward, specifically to a pleasurable event." When we combine anticipation with anxiety, the definition changes. Anticipatory anxiety is the anxiety we experience with the initial thought and anticipation of doing something. Now we are in a state of mind where we are still looking forward, but we are anticipating something bad happening. The truth is that the actual situation is never as bad or as anxiety-producing as the anticipation.

❀**Nothing is ever as bad as you expect it will be. The anticipation is most often the worst part.**

About twelve years ago, when I was just about completely recovered, I was approved as a speaker for a national organization dedicated to people with phobias and anxiety. I knew that I would be in the company of some prominent psychologists and psychiatrists, and that made me anxious. I went nuts writing my speech; I worked for six weeks prior to the lecture date, preparing my material. I was afraid I wouldn't be good enough. When I saw my name on the brochure beside all of the M.D.s and Ph.D.s, my mind started in.

What am I doing?
Who am I kidding?
Why am I going?
I can't do this.
What if I get up there and forget what I'm supposed to say?
What if I make a fool of myself?
What if the doctors judge me for not using the right clinical terms?
What if my presentation is too long?
What if it isn't long enough?
What if I get nervous and I can't get up there and do it?

My mind was going ninety miles an hour before I even left for the trip. To add to it all, there was quite a bit of tur-

bulence on the plane to San Francisco. Between the anticipation of my presentation and the rough flight, I was
pretty tense. When I arrived at the hotel, I signed up for an
early evening bus tour of San Francisco. Then, when I went
to check out the room where I would be presenting the
next day, I ran into a colleague. "Hi, Lucinda!" he said. "I
saw your name on the roster for 8:30 A.M. tomorrow. I
guess I know what you'll be doing tonight."

I smiled. "Well, actually, I'm taking a bus tour through
San Francisco." I thought it would be relaxing and take my
mind off my presentation.

"I can't believe you're taking a bus tour the night before
an 8:30 presentation. Boy, I'd never do that!" He walked
away, shaking his head.

That did it. Now I was really questioning myself. "What
if he's right? Maybe I should sit in my room all night and
go over my notes." But I knew the presentation like the
back of my hand. If anything, I was over-prepared! I
decided to trust my instincts, to go on the tour, relax and
have a wonderful time. Wasn't that a form of preparation
also?

I enjoyed the tour immensely. When I got back to my
room, I went to sleep with positive self-talk. "There's nothing to fear. These people don't know what I've written and
memorized, so they won't know if I say it correctly or not.
I'm not here to impress anybody. I'm here to give and to
share myself. They'll either appreciate it or they won't. I'll
just do my best." I dropped off to sleep with relative ease,
considering I had a lecture first thing in the morning.
Anybody would have a small level of anxiety and I com-
forted myself by remembering that.

I woke up in the morning and did my presentation. I
was well prepared, I was on a natural high, and I barely
even looked at my notes. I love to speak and I had fun,
speaking from my heart, sharing my personal experiences

and connecting with my audience. When the hour and a half was up, nobody wanted to leave, myself included. At the end of each talk, the audience was handed seminar evaluation forms for the particular speaker they had just heard. After everyone had left, I walked up to the woman who had collected the forms. "Do you think I could see my evaluations?" I asked her. I was curious and at the same time, a little bit apprehensive.

"Oh sure. Here," she said, grabbing a pile of papers off the desk and handing them to me. "These are yours." She handed me a pile. I looked at the first one. "This is the best presentation I've seen all weekend!" As I glanced at the evaluations they were full of fabulous comments, suggesting that my presentation be longer, that I come back every year and that there be more sessions like mine.

If I had had a positive "what-if" dialogue for the six weeks before my talk, it would have been empowering and accurate and I could have saved myself much anticipatory anxiety. It might have sounded like this:

"What if I do a great job?"

I did.

"What if this takes me to a whole new level in my career?"

It did.

"What if this gives me a whole new self-confidence about my speaking ability?"

That happened.

"What if I touch one person?"

I touched a lot of people and they touched me.

"What if exposing my own insecurities makes me seem more real to my audience and more approachable?"

They would hardly let me leave.

On my return flight home, I was so elated, satisfied, and filled with joy, I could have flown home without a plane!

Worst Case Scenarios

The first step in transforming your thoughts is getting in touch with them, exactly as they are. You have to recognize your "what-if" syndrome before you can change it. I call this "taking your thoughts to the worst case scenario."

❀**Most often, the worse thing that could happen isn't really all that bad or it never happens at all.**

Sarah, one of the women in my group, was afraid that when she became anxious, she would lose her mind. We all knew she wouldn't. Anxious people don't go crazy, but they nearly drive themselves crazy worrying about it.

"So if you lost your mind, what would happen?" I asked her one afternoon during a session.

"They'd put me in an insane asylum."

"Then?"

"They'd lock me up for the rest of my life and nobody would love me."

"Okay, then what?"

"They'd put me in a straitjacket?"

"Okay, and what if they did?"

"Well, I suppose they'd take it off me. Nobody lives in a straitjacket."

"And you'd stay there forever?"

"No, I'm sure my kids would get me out. They hate cooking for themselves."

We all laughed and someone in the group reminded Sarah that they don't put people with anxiety disorder in mental institutions or straitjackets. It was all negative fantasy. The important thing was that as Sarah spoke out her worst case scenario instead of repressing it, she began to see for herself that she was making it all up in her mind. She saw that she had blown it way out of perspective.

Time and again, worst case scenarios are just that: scenarios. There is no foundation or truth in them. One of the most popular fears is, "What if I have a panic attack and pass out?" In my twelve years of cofacilitating groups, no one in our groups ever passed out from a panic attack. And yet I hear people say, "What if I'm standing in line in an amusement park and I pass right out from fear?" "What if I'm driving and I pass out on the freeway and have a terrible accident?" The subsequent dialogue is always the same. Have you ever passed out? No. Then why do you think you're going to? No reason, it's just my fear.

❀ **Your fears are all about losing control. If you want to stay in control, stay in the present instead of projecting into the future.**

Be Here Now

Anticipating, whether we do it in a positive or a negative context, is always about the future. If we are anticipating, we are setting up expectations, preventing any possibility of spontaneity. Worrying about the past is another sure-fire method of keeping ourselves from enjoying the present moment, where freedom and happiness exist. As Carolyn Dickman, our education director at the Midwest Center, says, "Your present moment is very precious." It's all we have. When we're fearfully anticipating the future or obsessing about the past, we're wasting precious moments. How do we bring ourselves back to the present? Here's a series of questions you can ask yourself that will bring you back into the moment.

Who is here with me?
What am I touching?
What do I smell?

What do I hear?
What can I see?
What is around me?

Open your eyes and look around. Let your senses bring you back to exactly where you are. Give 100 percent of yourself to right now. As soon as you recognize the anticipatory thought process beginning, take a ten-second time out. Then start envisioning your worst case scenario. Try replacing the what-ifs with "so what-if."
"What if I have a panic attack right here in the mall?"
"I'll have to leave the store."
"So what if I walk out of the store?"
"I'll have to sit down and catch my breath."
"So what if I do that?"
"I might have to leave the mall."
So what if you have to leave the mall? It's no big deal. The mall isn't going anywhere. You can always shop at another time. What are you afraid of? Clothes aren't going to jump off the rack and hurt you, nothing is going to fall out of the sky and hit you on the head. Put everything into perspective. What could possibly happen that would make you feel bad, have a heart attack, lose your mind, or die? Nothing. So what if you're uncomfortable for an hour? No big deal. "But what if I embarrass myself? What if someone notices me?" People are too busy to notice you!

❀**The worst result of a panic attack is that you'll feel anxious, spacey, weird, or fuzzy in the head. Then you may be depressed and tired when it's all over. No big deal.**

One of the things that helped me the most was the knowledge that I could give myself permission to be anxious. When I got that bewildered feeling, I'd say to myself, "I'm feeling weird and spacey. It's no big deal. I'm going to just float with the feelings. I'm going to allow myself to feel this way and I'm even going to see the humor in it and laugh at myself a little. So what if I feel strange? I can still function fairly normally." I found that the more I anticipated panic and made a big deal out of it, the longer it stayed. The less upset I got by what I was feeling, the quicker it went away.

THE WALL

Feeling better doesn't require that you change your personality completely. You wouldn't want to, because many of your personality traits are assets. You can simply learn to use what you already have in a positive way. At the same time, you must face your worst fears, acknowledge them, and move forward in spite of them. Your complete recovery depends upon your willingness to challenge yourself. Then, when you've taken on a challenge and all your symptoms are in high gear, you may hit something I call the wall of anticipatory anxiety.

✤ **Anticipatory anxiety is a wall blocking you from achieving your goals. You have the ability to pass straight through it and claim your happiness.**

Hitting the wall is a great opportunity, one you've been waiting for your whole life! It's time to put one foot right through that wall, and then the other foot too. Now step out the other side. Doesn't it look better out here? It's time to move forward and do it anyway, in spite of your anxiety and fear. If you sit around and wait for the wall to disappear before you take action, you'll probably sit there forever.

A man named Mark came to group once to talk about a job offer. It was a job he had always wanted, but he was hesitant to accept the offer.

"What are you waiting for?" I asked him.

"I want to wait until I feel I little less anxious," he said.

"But you're not going to feel less anxious until you step through the wall of fear. Why don't you just take the job, let yourself experience all the feelings of anxiety and realize that you can do it anyway? Push yourself through the wall and do whatever it is you want to do in spite of the feelings of fear and anxiety. Then you'll realize that you survived and it wasn't as bad as you thought. And you'll have such a feeling of accomplishment!"

Mark did it. He took the job and stepped through his wall of anticipatory anxiety. When he returned to group the next week we asked him how it went.

"My first day was a challenge," he said. "My heart pounded, I broke out in a sweat, I thought for sure I was going to have a heart attack, and I didn't think I'd make it until 5:00, but I did! Each day it got easier."

Two months later, Mark had no more anxiety about his job. He was much stronger than before and he felt very proud of himself. He had learned that you can't put the cart before the horse. You have to take the first step, anxiety and all, and then allow the fear to dissipate. It doesn't work the other way around.

So many people procrastinate because of their anxiety, waiting for a time when it won't feel so bad, or they won't be so anxious, or worse yet, they wait for a time when their fear might be gone completely. "I'll start working on my driving when I get rid of my anxiety," or "I'll try flying when I don't have panic attacks any more," or "I'll go after that promotion once my anxiety is under control." When we know ourselves better, we understand that these excuses are a lack of self-acceptance. We are saying that a part of us isn't okay. It's not true. Wherever you are right now, however you feel in this moment, it's better than okay. You're on the verge of greatness! You have so much untapped potential, which you'll be able to utilize to the fullest advantage when you learn to accept yourself exactly as you are. That includes being anxious and anticipating, but doing it anyway!

Expect to feel anticipatory anxiety. Understand what it is. Push through the wall and do it anyway, whatever it is: driving, traveling, socializing, standing in lines, speaking, singing, dancing, writing, taking risks, changing careers, starting relationships, being assertive. JUST DO IT! Go out on the date. Go back to the shopping mall. Use your coping skills, choose a time when you're healthy, alert, rested, and positive, and get on that plane. Look at your pounding heart as a symbol of your excitement. Because it is!

Best Case Scenarios

What if you had a fear of heights and you stepped out on a balcony? Your fearful thoughts might be about jumping, falling, or feeling dizzy. But instead of thinking about the worst case scenario, what if you stopped yourself and started to imagine the best? It might go something like this.

What if I step through my wall of fear and go out on this balcony right now?

What if I admire the beautiful view and start to feel comfortable?

What if I feel immense joy at seeing such a gorgeous sight?

What if I end up liking heights?

What if I like being up high so much, I decide to fly and I take a trip to Europe?

Let yourself go into your wildest imagination. Have fun with it! Play with it! How far can you take it? It should be easy; you've developed a powerful imagination anticipating negative experiences. How about using it to anticipate positive ones? Let's go even further.

What if I ended up taking flying lessons?
What if I get my pilot's license?
What if I buy my own small airplane or helicopter?

Impossible, you say? I say, Not so! Not with all of your creative energy, imagination, and potential. When you step out on that balcony and face your anticipatory anxiety head on, you're on your way to overcoming your fears and living the life you've always wanted to live.

I remember years ago when David and I took a trip to the big island of Hawaii. We were given free vouchers to take a forty-five-minute helicopter ride over Wiapeo Valley. It sounded wonderful and I was really looking forward to it, but because I had never flown in a helicopter before, I was a little bit nervous. When we arrived at the airport, the pilot asked me if I had ever flown in a helicopter before.

"No, this is my first time," I said.

"Great, you can be my copilot!" he said with a smile. There were four passengers, myself, David, and another couple. They crawled in the back and lucky me, I crawled into the front seat beside the pilot. With glass surrounding me on all sides as well as under my feet, I felt suspended in midair as we rose straight up. The pilot handed us each a set of headphones. "Put them on," he told us. Intense drum music bellowed into our ears as we rose up, up, up, higher and higher over the Wiapeo Valley.

As you can imagine, right about this time I was feeling nervous, hovering in glass over a boundless valley, heading toward an ominous-looking set of mountains with Indian drum music vibrating in my ears. I like to talk when I'm nervous, but there was no chance! We topped the peak of the mountains and headed over the edge, when the pilot suddenly dropped the helicopter beneath the mountain crest. It felt like a couple of hundred feet, straight down! He was intensifying the already overwhelming sensation of falling into the deep crevices, thousands of feet below us.

We were so high and the terrain was so rugged and deep, it took my breath away. Spontaneously, I closed my eyes and my arm shot sideways, and I smacked the pilot in the stomach! He just smiled. He was enjoying my fear! My first thought was, "Help! I want off. I want out! Turn around!" But that was impossible. We couldn't go back and I realized it. I was at the point of no return. "If I'm going to die," I thought, "I might as well open my eyes to see where I am." I opened my eyes and looked in front of me. I had never seen such extraordinary beauty. I was in awe and my body slowly began to relax. What a thrill! What magnificence! The pilot felt my ease and continued gliding in and out of places that most people would never see. He teased the edges of spectacular waterfalls, flying almost to their edge and then quickly back out again.

I immersed myself in the beauty, remembering the intense fear I had felt just minutes before. If I could have, I would have "gotten out" of this and missed it; the experience of a lifetime. I wondered how many times I had allowed my fear and anticipation to stop me, just before I got to the good stuff.

When I got off the helicopter, I was exhilarated! "I loved it!" I said to David. "I could fly a helicopter! Let's get one some day," I told him.

Do you see? Anything is possible! I suggest you step through that wall of anticipatory anxiety, push yourself to the point of no return and then relax and enjoy the ride. Whether it's flying in a plane, speaking in front of a group, or taking a trip to the drug store, it could be the experience of a lifetime! It's time to look at your life from a different point of view. When you face your fears, you can use the confidence you'll gain to be the best that you can be. So dream the most beautiful dreams that you can; take them to the end of the world and beyond. Once you begin, there is no limit to the things you can accomplish!

CHAPTER 6

GUILT, ANGER, AND BLAME:
So Whose Fault Is It Anyway?

Dear Lucinda,

I know I'm a good person but I am riddled with guilt, self-doubt and anger all the time. I know all this stems from my upbringing. I've been this way since I was 9 or 10 and as I grew up, my parents kept putting me down. My back-ground was very dysfunctional but I am a survivor. Going to my family for support was like digging a grave. I haven't seen my father in 12 years and my mother finally sought help, but died of cancer before it could really do her any good. Thank God she passed some of her new knowledge on to me. She was my link to a positive path and she's gone.

I have done very well for myself but I feel guilty for it. I want to love myself, I want to have friends and trust people, but I am so afraid all the time.

Debby

❧ *Every winner has scars.*

—Herbert Casson

GUILT ATTACK

During my first years in college, I was pushing myself very hard. I was doing what it took to maintain a four point average, I was working full time, and I was in a relationship that was not supportive. My body was exhausted, my emotions were stressed to the max, and I needed a break. I decided to go to my parents' house for the weekend to get away. At this time, I hadn't a clue that I had anxiety disorder and I had no understanding of my body symptoms. I didn't know how overloaded I really was; I just knew that I didn't feel very well and I headed home to my parents.

I was in my old bedroom trying to take a nap when I bolted straight up in bed. Everything I had ever done that I considered bad passed through my mind. Actions I felt I shouldn't have done, things I shouldn't have said, thoughts I shouldn't have had. I was panicked, my heart was pumping, and I couldn't catch my breath. I was having an anxiety attack fueled by guilt.

I rushed out of the bedroom and flew downstairs. I remember standing there in the living room, interrupting a heated discussion between my parents. I stared at the red-flowered wallpaper, feeling disoriented and weird, breathing heavy, with no idea why I was standing there. I only knew I was scared to death. I looked at my mother and told her, "You've got to take me to the hospital! I'm losing my mind."

My mother and I got into my car. Maybe it was the familiarity of my old Datsun 280Z, but for whatever reason, the only place I felt safe was behind the wheel of that car. I slowly drove around the block and I talked and talked. I poured out everything that was in my heart, everything I felt guilty about. When I was through, my anxiety had dissipated and we went back to the house.

As I think back, this was one of the most severe panic attacks I ever had, solely generated by guilt and fear that I had been harboring for my entire life. What had I done that was so bad? Nothing!

Guilt has no real purpose, but people with anxiety tend to have a lot of it anyway. It can be related to things that happened when we were children, due to dysfunctional families, child abuse, molestation, separation from a loved one, or other environmental stressors. Some of the people in my group actually thought their anxiety was their just deserts for what they had done or been through in their lives. Anxiety was the punishment; guilt was the generator. They were harboring it as a way of paying themselves back because they thought they didn't deserve to be happy. Of course, this is completely untrue. We all crave and deserve happiness, but guilt keeps us from it.

There is an infinite list of things that we can feel guilty about. I felt guilty about having an alcoholic parent, as if it were my fault. As a child, I felt guilty about being poor, and, as an adult, about not being the perfect student, girlfriend, employee. Were you abusive toward someone in your past, either verbally or physically? Do you still feel guilty about it? Were you the object of someone else's abuse? Do you still feel responsible? Most likely, whatever happened to you as a child wasn't your fault, but you've been carrying around the guilt anyway. Did you ever do something deliberately to hurt another person, and now you really regret it? Did you say something horrible to a sister or brother? Did you lose your temper with someone who passed away and you never had a chance to apologize? These are a few of the many things that can generate guilt.

If you had a pad and paper with you and kept track of each time you felt guilty, a conservative estimate would be that we feel guilty at least ten times in a single day. If you continued to track it, I'll bet you'd find that you feel recurring guilt about things that you do on a daily basis.

There are so many things, both large and small, that cause us to be hard on ourselves:

- I don't spend enough time with my children.
- I work too much and don't give my wife enough attention.
- I wasn't nice to my mother yesterday.
- I snapped at my employee.
- I forgot to return a phone call.
- I shouldn't be smoking.
- I can't seem to control my weight anymore.
- I don't give my husband enough sex.
- I don't listen to my daughter.
- I didn't go to college.
- I didn't work as hard as I should have today.

Guilt Is a Cover-up for Low Self-Esteem

The guilt that you have about something you did is a cover-up for the way you feel about yourself. Maybe deep down inside, you think that if people really knew who you were, how insecure you can be, how anxious you get, how depressed you sometimes are, they wouldn't like you. You may feel that at times you're a mean, selfish, inconsiderate person, secretly harboring resentment because of all you do for others, and this may make you feel guilty.

Whatever the source of your guilt, the outcome will be the same. Whether your particular guilt arises from the kind of husband you think you are, how you function as a parent, how you're treating your own parents, how you're running your business, or what thoughts you're carrying, it all has to do with low self-esteem.

✼**Wherever your guilt is coming from, it all breaks down to the same disempowering labels. "I'm a bad person. I did something wrong. I should be punished."**

Guilt justifies your unhappiness and suffering. It justifies your reasons for having an unpleasant past. When you're feeling guilty, you may be telling yourself, "I was unkind to my wife, so I don't deserve to be happy. I'm really not a very nice person and that's why nothing goes right for me." If you hurt someone, it's easy to mistakenly think that when they see your guilt, they'll know you're paying for what you did. However, it never works that way. You suffer and they get a grouchy partner, filled with shame, who has become depressing to be around.

If guilt feels so bad and brings on so much negativity, then why don't we just let go of it? It sounds logical and perfectly simple, but like any growth-oriented experience, releasing guilt is a process that involves awareness, dealing with resistance, and eventually self-acceptance and compassion.

As surprising as it may sound, feeling good may bring on a tremendous amount of anxiety. That's because deep down inside, we feel we don't deserve happiness. Guilt is a way of explaining our unhappiness, justifying it and keeping ourselves in it. For some of us, feeling bad is so comfortably familiar, we almost prefer it to feeling better. The decision to move beyond guilt and allow yourself to feel good requires some courage.

Once again, it's one foot in front of the other. We can move slowly, by taking one step at a time toward releasing guilt. Let's begin by taking a serious look at what you actually did and how you feel about it. Here are some questions to ask yourself.

- If you hurt someone, was it deliberate? Or did you act out of fear or a need you thought you had at the time? Was it your own pain that motivated you to hurt someone else?
- Was the hurt you caused an accident? Perhaps you never meant for it to happen. Some things happen due to circumstances beyond our control. Was this one of those things?
- Did you do something that was really so terrible? If so, by whose standards?
- Can you make it right? Can you change it, correct it, or apologize for it?
- Isn't the guilt you feel nonproductive? Are you beating yourself up and making yourself miserable? Or are you being realistic, feeling regret and remorse and taking steps to develop a sensible strategy for change, forgiveness, and acceptance? Can you find a way to forgive yourself and move beyond it?

It is easy to believe that someone else is causing your guilt. Is there someone in your life who is trying to shift responsibility onto you by deliberately trying to make you feel guilty? Do they know that guilt works with you? If they have successfully pushed your buttons in the past, they may continue to do so, in order to get a desired reaction from you. It is not that they are bad people. Often, it is an unconscious game they are playing.

Unfortunately, those of us with anxiety disorder are susceptible to guilt, because we are so analytical and sensitive. We tend to dwell on negative thoughts; we dissect what we did, trying desperately to justify our actions, all the time feeling more and more guilty. We want so much to be liked by everyone that we tend to be people pleasers. We don't like conflict or feelings of disapproval. That is why so many of us have a hard time saying no.

It is up to you to recognize when someone is putting blame on you. The game stops when you stop allowing it. It is your choice. Take a good look and decide if you are choosing to feel guilt over someone else's accusations. Are you letting someone push your buttons? Do you want him to continue to manipulate you in this way? Are you willing to stand up for yourself and not feel guilty? The truth is that no one can make you feel guilty. You choose guilt for yourself.

Most people get secondary gains from feeling guilty. It's a great way to fill up the space in the present and distract yourself from an immediate solution. Then you don't have to think about changing. I've had a lot of guilt in my life, and take it from me, nothing worthwhile can come of it.

Cultivating an Attitude of Forgiveness

None of us is perfect. We all have past situations that we wish we had handled differently. Being guilty and giving yourself a hard time will only cause more negative feelings. Remorse, on the other hand, is a productive human response, completely different from guilt. Remorse leads to forgiveness. If we want to understand what we did and ways to change, we must learn to cultivate an attitude of forgiveness toward ourselves. Without it, being honest will be too painful.

How can we take an honest look at our actions, if we're waiting in the wings to criticize and scold ourselves? Only if we know how to forgive ourselves will we find the courage to be honest with ourselves and others. People who continually blame and persecute themselves blow their actions way out of proportion. Wouldn't you be willing to forgive someone else for doing something she sincerely regretted? Why aren't you willing to forgive yourself?

✢ **We can't change the past. What's done is done. If we want to get healthy, we must learn to forgive both ourselves and others. Then we can begin to let go of guilt and move forward.**

Review your answers to the questions on page 118 and then follow these steps to learn to let go and forgive yourself.

• **Analyze with an open mind whatever you consider your wrongdoing to have been.**

Be as kind to yourself and as realistic as possible. It may be difficult at first, but it gets easier with practice.

• **If your wrongdoing is something you can apologize for, do so.**

Do not be concerned with how much time has passed. Whenever you let someone know you're sorry, you'll be amazed at the sense of relief you'll feel. You're apologizing to release yourself from the bondage of guilt, but remember: you can't control someone else's reaction. It may not be the one you wanted, but your reaction is what's important. When you apologize to someone else, be the first one to accept it.

• **If your guilt feels unsurpassable, allow yourself to have it, but set a time limit.**

How long will you let yourself suffer for your mistake? An hour? A day? Certainly not any longer than that! Take some time alone and reflect on what happened. What can you do to ensure you won't repeat it? What positive lessons are available through your mistake? Can you give yourself credit for being honest, for growing and learning, for becoming a more responsible person? Doesn't this sound better than making yourself feel bad and sick?

- **Adopt an "oh, well, I'm human" attitude.**

This gives you the freedom to take chances and make mistakes. Everyone makes mistakes. Smart people forgive themselves. Then they can learn from their errors and have the courage to try again.

- **Let go.**

Say out loud to yourself, "I forgive myself for that. It's over and done. I'm not going to waste precious moments by dwelling on the past. I choose to be happy now."

A woman in one of our groups whom I'll call Mary was married for a few years in her early twenties to her high school sweetheart. "We were never really right for each other," she told me, "and as we matured, we grew apart. I felt like a failure when we got divorced and I carried around a lot of guilt for a long time. 'Why didn't it work out?' I kept asking myself. 'What did I do wrong? What did he do wrong?'"

As she talked about her feelings with the group, I suggested she take a big step. "What do you think about seeing your ex-husband to apologize to him and to forgive him? But, Mary, remember to choose your words carefully. Don't put blame on him. Don't bring up specifics or make him defensive. In fact, it might be preferable in this situation that he doesn't know what you're doing."

"I'd really like to do that," she said, "but I don't know what to tell him."

"Just say you're sorry for what you both went through.

You don't have to ask his forgiveness, but know in your heart that this is your apology and that you're forgiving him."

"Okay. It's time," she said.

She did it. She went to see him and told him about her realization that it wasn't his fault and it wasn't her fault. It just wasn't meant to be. He stood there and listened without saying much and that was okay. She said he got sarcastic exactly the way he used to get, but she didn't let it bother her.

"I simply said what I needed to say and I left," she told us in group the next week. "I didn't have any expectations about how my feelings would be received and it worked. I've been having recurring dreams about him and now they've stopped." Mary smiled broadly. She looked like she had dropped a tremendous weight she had been carrying for a long time, and now it was over.

THE ANGER ATTACK

There was a young woman in one of my groups who had a problem with anger. She came in one night very concerned and embarrassed about an incident that had happened the night before, involving her fiancé. "He had gotten to my place late," she said. "I had made a great dinner and while I was waiting for him, I began to get angry. The food was getting cold, I had an exceptionally bad day and I really needed to talk to him. The later it got, the more angry I got. When he finally got to my apartment I exploded. I said horrible things and used bad language. I was like a time bomb ready to go off."

Mary was having an anxiety attack, fueled with anger. It really scared her because she felt so completely out of control, secretly worrying that there might be something wrong with her. She said that this had happened many times before. "After a tirade, I feel as if I've been abusive. I'm embarrassed and ashamed and I have terrible guilt."

We can't discuss guilt without bringing up anger and blame. As a matter of fact, they are all so closely intertwined, it's difficult to discuss any one of these difficult emotions without eventually touching on the other two members of the "gruesome threesome."

There are various ways people express their anger and most of them are ineffective. There was another particularly angry woman who came to group. She had wanted her husband to work overtime so they'd have money to build a spare room onto their house. She had really pushed him into taking on extra work, but once he did, she was angry that he was working such long hours. When she complained about her situation, we said to her, "Now wait just a minute here! You were the one who wanted the spare room."

The next week, she arrived at group very excited. She could hardly wait to tell us what she had done. "Normally, when Alan gets home, I have his dinner waiting. I greet him at the door, give him a beer and have dinner with him. But on Friday night, I wasn't there to meet him at all."

"Where were you?" I asked her. "Did you go out?"

"Oh no," she said smugly. "I was home but I stayed in my bedroom. In fact, I stayed there the whole weekend and gave him the silent treatment. I never saw him or spoke to him. I really showed him!"

"Do you have a television in your bedroom?" I asked her.

"No," she answered. "It's in the living room."

"Do you have a radio?"

"No."

"How about a telephone?"

"No."

"What on earth did you do for an entire weekend?"

"I read magazines and cleaned closets and just hung out."

"And what did he do?"

"Oh, I heard him talking on the phone and watching television. He mowed the lawn, drank a few beers, and napped on the couch. I just stayed right there in the bedroom and ruined his weekend!"

We all exchanged glances. It sounded as if her husband was having a wonderful and relaxing time while she was angry and miserable, cooped up in her bedroom for several days in a row. He was probably secretly grateful that she was not in his face nagging him. So, whose weekend did she ruin anyway?

Think before you react.

I can't stress enough how important this is. People with anxiety are often seeking immediate gratification in the form of spontaneous release. This tends to create reaction before thought. How many times have you been angry over something you absolutely couldn't change or control? How many hours, days, or weeks have you wasted, wallowing in angry, nonproductive feelings?

Some of us have repressed our emotions for so long, we hardly know whether or not we're angry. Anger is a tough one; those of us who are anxiety-prone are afraid that if we admit to our anger, nobody will like us. But this is counterproductive. The only way to let go of anger is first to acknowledge it. Then, once we know how angry we truly are or are not, we can take the appropriate steps to heal ourselves and become happier people.

Your Right to Be Angry

Do you consider anger to be bad? It isn't. Did you know that it is normal to have it and that there's a way to use it effectively? Most people haven't learned this skill and aren't good at utilizing anger in a productive way. The reason we have a hard time expressing our anger is our strong need for approval. We want to be liked at all costs. If we show someone we're angry, they might think poorly of us or they might judge us as being out of control. To someone with anxiety disorder, that's the ultimate disgrace. So we only show our friends and coworkers our good side. We keep the rest to ourselves out of fear of rejection or disapproval, and this can be a problem. Do you trust someone who won't show you their feelings and insecurities? Doesn't it make you want to withdraw from them because somehow you know they're not being real. If somebody is a true friend or lover, they won't stop loving you because you get angry.

A great deal of anxiety comes from built-up hostility. When we are too afraid to say something that we need to say, we're setting ourselves up for problems. You don't have to repress your feelings, no matter what they are. When you talk intimately to someone, do you feel comfortable enough to show your anger and disagree in a mature way?

Highly sensitive people tend to be easily irritated. They tend to overreact to the various frustrations and disappointments that are a normal part of life. I remember a young mother who couldn't control her anger. "I seem to do okay at work," she said. "But when I get home, I lose it over the stupidest things. I yell at my kids for making a mess or not doing their homework. And I think they're learning how to be angry from watching me. They yell at each other and sometimes they seem to have bad attitudes. I'm afraid their memories of childhood will be about a mother who screamed and yelled all the time."

As she talked I could feel her embarrassment and guilt. She didn't like herself this way. She continued. "My poor husband is the one I really jump on. If he doesn't get the right thing at the grocery store or he leaves a mess in the kitchen, I unload on him. Especially right before my period. I swear, my whole personality changes then. I get irritable, insecure, anxious, and depressed. I'm so moody and I take it out on my kids and my husband. I can't seem to help it."

If you can recognize yourself as someone who is prone to quick irritation or verbal explosions, make a strong commitment to change your negative responses into something more controlled and effective. When you're angry, I suggest you ask yourself the following questions:

- **Stop and think. Take a time out. Whether you stop for ten seconds or 24 hours, it will allow you to be clear about your desired outcome. What do you really want to happen as a result of expressing your feelings? Do you want someone else to understand that you're hurt and you need to discuss the issue? Do you want to resolve a problem or do you want to make someone else feel bad, too? If so, why? Isn't that nonproductive?**
- **Is your anger useful in this situation? Wouldn't you rather communicate and problem solve? Will you use your anger to help produce satisfying results or will it just make everybody feel worse?**
- **Was the person who hurt you having a personal problem or were they really angry at you? Are you taking it personally?**
- **Are you angry about a situation over which you have no control and that you can't change? If it's stupid or pointless, wouldn't it be better to redirect your energy and let go, instead of wasting your precious time?**
- **If you're staying angry at someone, hoping to make them feel bad, aren't you giving them an additional hold on you and prolonging your own bad feelings?**

A Ph.D. who came to group was caring for his ninety-three-year-old mother. He had moved her in with him because she was senile and couldn't do anything for herself. He had spent the better part of his life trying to be who his mother had wanted him to be. All he wanted was for her to say that she loved him and was proud of him. She never had, and now she didn't even know who he was anymore. He knew there was no chance of ever getting what he wanted, and yet he was holding on to his anger. The truth was that even in her senile state, his mother was still controlling him. His anger was unproductive, it was draining his life, and until he made a decision to drop it, it would give him nothing but grief.

If you find yourself getting angry standing in line at the post office or waiting in a traffic jam, don't do it to yourself. It's a waste of time. Life is too short. The overreactive personality type has been linked to heart disease, strokes, and various other illnesses and complications. Don't be an overreactor.

When you have rationally considered your situation and decided that there is a valid reason to express your anger, you can do it in a mature way that will give you the desired results. This is called effective assertive response.

- **Start expressing your anger with "I" messages.**

Don't ever say to someone, "You hurt me and you made me angry." That will only make them defensive. If you don't accuse, you'll have a better chance of being heard. Instead of saying, "You did this to me," try saying, "This is why I'm upset, this is what's bothering me. What do you think we can do about this or what can I do about that?"

- **Keep your voice calm. Don't scream.**

If you start yelling at someone, they'll feel attacked. It'll end up in an argument and the winner will be the one with the most aggressive personality. That probably won't be you, since you are accustomed to being nice so you'll be liked. Even if it is you, whoever wins the fight doesn't really win. Nobody wins because everybody ends up feeling hurt and betrayed and there is no resolution.

If you need to get out your physical violence, kick a ball, beat on a pillow, run a mile. If you need to get out your verbal violence, yell in the car or in a private place where you won't frighten anyone. Don't attack another person, physically or verbally. If you do, their survival instincts will automatically kick in. They'll close down and they won't hear a word you're saying. Their mind will be occupied in figuring out how to come back at you.

- **If you have to point out someone's shortcomings, think of something positive to say to them first.**

Before you speak, think about something they did recently that you felt good about. Then you can start your confrontation with, "You really helped me a lot this week and I appreciate it." Now you've got their attention. Then address the real issue in "I" messages. "*I* need to talk about something that happened today that *I'm* uncomfortable with."

Tell them how you feel without raising your voice. Watch your body language. Maintain good eye contact. Don't be wordy, don't go on and on. Speak succinctly, get to the point and don't rub it in.

- **Wait quietly for their response.**

This is hard to do because you may feel anxious and want to keep talking, but give your friend a chance. He has feelings, too, and you may not be aware of them. There are always at least two views on every situation. Make a sincere effort to put yourself in his shoes and understand his feelings. When he is talking, listen. Don't interrupt and don't respond until he's finished. This will help you to focus on what he's saying. Wouldn't you want the same consideration? Isn't your goal to be a better problem-solver? This is how you do it!

- **End the discussion on a positive note.**

You can validate him. "Hey, I really appreciate your taking the time to listen to me." If he feels appreciated for having listened to you, he will probably be open to this type of communication at another time. Then, you'll both feel more secure and you'll have less anxiety the next time you feel angry. Isn't that the whole point?

Good rule of thumb: Always try to go to bed with a clear, calm, peaceful mind. Clear the air so that you can start the next day or even the next moment with a positive, self-loving attitude. Having a peaceful mind is a decision that you make. I like to use Scarlett O'Hara's positive self-talk from the last scene of *Gone With the Wind*: "I'll think about it tomorrow." Try it at night. It works. Tell yourself you're putting the anger or concern aside and you'll think about it tomorrow. Maybe by tomorrow, you'll forget about it!

Misery Loves Company

Did you know that in most cases, other people's anger has nothing to do with you? Are you taking it personally anyway? When someone is in a bad mood, they want to make someone else feel bad, too. There's an old expression, "Misery loves company." That's when someone goes out of their way to enroll you in their anger and misery. If someone who has turmoil in his life is taking it out on you, step back. Take a ten-second time out. Say to yourself, "I wonder if Jim had a bad day at the office." Or, "What's going on in Eleanor's life that's making her so angry at herself?" Then let yourself off the hook by saying, "I'm not going to take this personally. It isn't worth it and besides that, it has nothing to do with me."

❧ **If someone gets angry at you, you must decide how to react and respond.**

Here are some examples of how someone or something makes you angry, and some possible responses that will bring creative positive change.

• **My father makes me angry. Even though I'm CEO of my own company, he still treats me like a child. He criticizes me constantly and tells me how to run my business.**

I've told myself that this is how he is and he isn't going to change. I told him in a controlled tone of voice that I didn't appreciate his remarks. He seemed shocked. I felt guilty at first, but now I feel better and stronger for it.

• **I went to the pharmacy to get a prescription filled and the pharmacist couldn't fill it because his computer was down. I got irritated.**

I could have just relaxed and come back later. There was nothing he could do. I overreacted and made myself upset about something I couldn't control.

• **I wanted to go to a city a few hours away to buy some special tools. I wanted my wife to go along because I was uncomfortable at the thought of driving that far alone. She didn't want to go and said so. I got angry and accused her of not wanting me to get better.**

I used anger as a motivation. "I'll show her!" I thought to myself and I took the trip alone. It was the best thing I could have done. Sure I was nervous, but I did it. The feelings of accomplishment were fabulous. As for my wife, she didn't want to go and she had that right. I think she also wanted me to try it on my own so I could become independent again.

Are you angry at yourself and taking it out on another person? If you are, take a ten-second time out. Say to yourself, "Wait a minute. I'm not really mad at Janice. I'm angry at how I handled the situation at work today." Then you can take your wife aside and tell her, "Look, Janice. I'm not mad at you. I'm sorry I acted that way. It's just been a bad day and I didn't handle an important meeting very well. It really has nothing to do with you."

When you can be responsible for your own anger, when you can recognize your errors and forgive yourself, then you've really grown.

THE BLAME ATTACK

After one of my recent seminars, I spoke to a man in his late thirties who I'll call Bill. He waited until everyone had left, and then he had his mother wait out in the hall while he talked with me about "his" anxiety.

"Both my mother and my father have anxiety disorder," he told me. "I work with my father and he makes me anxious. He's demanding and difficult to work for and I have to be with him every day. He's always a nervous wreck and on edge."

"Have you ever thought about taking a different job where you wouldn't have to work with your father?" I asked him.

He gave me all sorts of reasons why that wasn't an option. He went on for twenty minutes, talking about his father's and mother's problems.

"Why don't you stop talking about them and tell me about you," I suggested.

He looked at me as if I just wasn't getting it. "But they are my problem!" he moaned in frustration. As I listened to him talk, I thought about how far from recovery this man was because in his mind, his problems were his parents' fault. Even then, in his late thirties, although his parents could no longer control him, he was letting them.

His mother entered the room and, overhearing his remarks about her and her husband, began to get defensive. The debate escalated. Bill got anxious and paced the floor. He began taking short deep breaths. He started to sweat. He was having an anxiety attack fueled with blame. He was convinced that his parents caused his anxiety. Until he could let go of the blame, he would have a difficult time healing.

Blame is something we learn at a very young age. I see it already programmed into children at school and in the neighborhood. A little boy fell down and when he went crying to his big brother, he was asked, "Who made you cry? Who did it to you? Whose fault is it?" It's almost instinctual.

Unless we get a handle on it, we can carry that programming with us through the rest of our lives. So what's your biggest blame, the reason you think you've been held back? What or who do you blame for your pain and anxiety? So whose fault is it anyway?

My biggest blame, far and away, was my father. The fact that he was an alcoholic was my excuse for my "have-nots"—the things I didn't have or felt I couldn't accomplish. I spent the better part of my life blaming him when things didn't go my way. When I didn't go to college right away, or I didn't have the money I needed, or I wasn't happy, or I wasn't going after my dreams, or I didn't get the job I wanted, or the boyfriend I wanted, subconsciously I thought it was because of my father. Once I grew up and came to realize that nobody was interested in my excuses, I also realized that until I forgave him, I'd be tied to the reason for my unhappiness and, therefore, tied to my unhappiness.

If you are your biggest blame, you're still a little bit off the track, but you're closer. If you can say, "I'm the reason for my 'have-nots,'" you're still blaming, but at least you're not projecting it out there on somebody or something you can't change. When you accept responsibility for your own discontent and unhappiness, you're on the way to controlling the only thing you really have control over—yourself.

SO WHOSE FAULT IS IT ANYWAY?

The truth is that nobody's to blame.

❀**It's nobody's fault that you're anxious, but you're the only one who can help you overcome it.**

If you want to spend the rest of your life blaming someone else for why you're not happy, why you don't have peace of mind, why you're not successful, why you're not healthy or thin or why you can't quit smoking or have a good relationship or get the job you want, or why you can't overcome your anxiety, you might as well put this book down.

On the other hand, if you're willing to stop blaming your father, your teacher, your husband or wife or child and say, "It's nobody's fault that I'm the way that I am. I want to change my life and I have the courage, the power, and the energy to do it," then I'd like to congratulate you. You're on the path to releasing yourself from guilt, anger, and blame, and taking responsibility for your own fulfillment and peace of mind. Recovery is just around the next curve.

❧ PART 2

RECOVERY

CHAPTER 7

TAKING RESPONSIBILITY FOR THE WAY YOU FEEL FOR THE REST OF YOUR LIFE

❦ *Our greatest power is the power to choose. We can decide where we are, what we do, and what we think. No one can take the power to choose away from us. It is ours alone. We can do what we want to do. We can be who we want to be.*

—AUTHOR UNKNOWN

Dear Lucinda,

Wow! Have I come a long way! I teach music to four-year-olds through eighth graders. I teach a positive living course at the hospital. It is a very popular course and the pay is excellent. I teach Sunday school to a 30+ class. I found this letter I had written about myself before I took your program and I couldn't believe it was me! I denied my negative feelings. I blocked out my anger and depression with alcohol. I let aggressive people walk all over me. I obsessively thought about weight, drinking and smoking but I didn't correct them. I have learned to slow down, be less concerned about what other people think, be proud of my opinions, have full confidence in myself, see problems as challenges, be assertive and in control of my life, deal with life more realistically, eat right, exercise and not be afraid of my thoughts. I was afraid of [everything] and now I am not. I hope my story can encourage others.

Tammy

I remember several years ago when I made the decision to write a book. I had all kinds of reasons why I shouldn't, wouldn't, couldn't. After all, what did I know about writing a book? How would I even begin?

One weekend, I was at a speaker's conference with a friend of mine, Henriette Klauser, Ph.D., who is an acclaimed author and writing instructor. The conference was a stimulating event with lots of talented professionals including speakers, teachers, students, and artists. All types of motivated, excited people, all wound up with high-powered energy.

On Saturday evening, Henriette and I were up late, talking and sharing ideas, when I told her that I wanted to write a book. It would include my personal experiences with anxiety, but mostly it would be about enabling other people to help themselves. Henriette was supportive and encouraging; she suggested I sit right down and write a little bit in the lobby of our hotel before calling it a night.

"What?" I said. "I didn't mean right now! It's too late. I'm too tired. And I haven't a clue how to do it right."

Henriette smiled, knowingly. "Just begin," she said. "Start writing."

"But I'm too tired. I have to wake up early, I have to go to the bathroom. I have to..."

I stopped talking and started writing:

Excuses. Which excuses will I use today and for which pro-
crastinations? Which times will I plunge through and keep
pushing myself and then...keep pushing myself a little further until it maybe even hurts a little? Until I get to the meat
of it.

Maybe writing is kind of like riding my exercise bike in
the morning. Once I made the decision to exercise, I
began... The first morning I was motivated.

Then ten minutes into it I became fatigued. I started to
sweat and wondered how much longer I could push
myself.

Fifteen minutes into it, I became very aware of my
breathing, the dampness of my body, my strong desire to
give in, give up.

Twenty minutes into it, I wondered how I will muster up
the energy and determination and self-motivation to do this
again tomorrow.

But then a gradual process began to happen. I began to
feel confident in my ability to pursue and maintain. "How
did I go this far?" I thought. I began to feel stronger physically and mentally, somehow proud of the sweat on my
neck, back and face. I began to feel as if I had conquered
something inside of myself.

I'll ride again this evening. Maybe I'll add more exercises
to my regime tomorrow, maybe I'll watch my diet more
closely. Look at me! Look at me! I am doing it! WOW!

"Could it be the same way with writing?" I thought, as
my pen kept inadvertently capturing my thoughts on
paper. "Could this be the way it is with so many of life's
challenges?" I have learned that most things of value don't
come easy. Especially growth-oriented experiences that
involve work and change. You can't expect to be excited
about doing them at first. Not until you've really gotten
involved. Not until you've started the wheels rolling, let
the sweat drip down your forehead, pushed yourself
beyond that middle point where you wonder if you can

continue, until you finally reach the point where you are so involved and excited, you wonder if you can stop. From this place comes true motivation, determination, and absolute commitment to keep going. Here is where true accomplishment lies. The payoff is the sense of pride and self-confidence that comes when you take control and change your life.

Making the decision to take action doesn't always feel good. Sometimes it's scary. Sometimes it creates anxiety. You ask yourself, "Does this mean I'll have to do something? Does this mean I'll have to work hard at something? Does this mean I'll have to commit to something, challenge myself or change?" If you want to change your life, you must start by changing yourself.

❀ **Sensitive people like us don't like change. But if we want to grow, change we must.**

I remember the first time I took responsibility for the way I was feeling by changing the way I responded to something. I was singing professionally and I had been dating David for six months. I loved him very much but I didn't want to admit it. Not to him, not to myself. I didn't want to be that vulnerable. He was so different from me at that time. He was so relaxed and fun-loving. Nothing seemed to bother him. He lived in the moment. I was twenty-four years old and full of anxiety. I had a hard time expressing my feelings and although no one suspected anything, I was experiencing severe panic attacks everywhere I went. I was singing professionally and I would panic on stage. I would panic in the car when we went on the road, but I didn't tell anybody. I didn't even consider talking about it; I had been having these anxious feelings for so long, I had adjusted to them.

It was January 1981, in the lounge of the Holiday Inn in

Toledo, Ohio. The room was packed. I had just walked off the stage feeling overheated, anxious, and claustrophobic. My chest was tight; I felt as if I were choking. The walls were closing in and I needed to get out, take a break and get some fresh air. As I headed for the door, David was the first person I saw. I had met him during my first week performing with the band. My group performed quite a lot in the Midwest and since I had just ended a long, unhealthy relationship, I thought this would be a great way to meet new people. As much as I enjoyed David and liked spending time with him, I still felt a desire to date other people. Initially I resented the commitment required to start a new relationship. There he was, waiting for me as usual. I was simultaneously relieved and annoyed to see him.

I opened the exit door, hoping David would follow me because I needed the company. We walked swiftly outside and headed straight for my car. David let me drive because he knew that was the only way I felt comfortable.

David didn't understand why I often acted this way and neither did I. I couldn't explain my fear of closed-in places, my recurring panic and nervousness, my unexplainable bouts of anger and mood swings, but they were very real. At that moment, I was in full-blown flight mode and I had only one thing in mind: to start up the car and get moving.

Although we were finally in motion, I couldn't relax. I needed to release the tension somehow. Unfortunately for David, I directed my tension to him. "Why do you always have to come and see me perform? I think I need some space," I said. David remained silent while I said many things that I really didn't mean, desperately trying to feel in control. Thinking back, I can almost hear my heart screaming on the inside, "Help! I don't like myself right now. I'm acting mean. I'm sorry. It's not your fault. I just feel bad and I don't know how to make it stop." Instead of letting my heart speak, I kept feeding him negative emotions and strong messages about my independence. When I finally glanced over at David, his eyes were sad, filled with shock and hurt. He didn't respond for fear of making me angrier, but what was there to say?

David loved me in spite of myself. Did I love myself in spite of myself? Not that night. In my attempt to make David feel bad, I suddenly was feeling bad about myself. What a rude awakening this was. I was completely bewildered by my stupid remarks. "You idiot," I thought to myself. "Look at him. Look how much he loves you. Look how much you've hurt him." Something different was happening in my mind at that moment; I was questioning myself in a new way. Did I want to spend the rest of my life like this, blaming others for my pain, blaming past situations for my anxiety? Deep down, I seemed to know that if I was going to change, it had to start then, at that moment. David hadn't done anything to make me angry. He just loved me and wanted to be with me. Plain and simple. I felt like a warrior without an adversary.

Then I did something I hadn't done in a long time. I took responsibility. I apologized. "I'm sorry, David," I said. "I'm wrong and I'm being a jerk. I feel awful right now and I don't know why. This feeling scares me and makes me want to run, to react somehow and even get mad if that's what it takes to feel more in control. I'm so sorry I hurt you." I waited in silence for his response, wondering if he would take advantage of my vulnerability. He didn't. David put his arms around me and held me. "It's okay," he said. "I'm here for you." What a relief to express my fear and insecurity and still be loved! On this cold, snowy night in Toledo, for the first time in my life, I learned about taking responsibility, and about the sense of relief and the feelings of fear that come with it. On one hand it felt so right, on the other it felt so scary. Would this make me too vulnerable? Would it take away my power?

Thinking back, I see that my anxiety got worse when I started dating David because, for the first time, I felt safe. Although I didn't realize it at the time, I must have known subconsciously that I could finally let go. I could let it out and deal with it and someone would be there to catch me. Often, when we know we need to deal with something difficult, we hold it in and wait until we have some type of support system in place to help us cope.

When my sister Donna found out she had cancer, she didn't deal with it in the first few days. Instead of letting herself cry or lose control, she became depressed and distant. A few days after her diagnosis, Mom and I made the trip to Louisville to be with her. We were a close family, so once her support system was surrounding her, she let go and temporarily lost control. On a subconscious level I believe she'd been waiting until we were all there, until her support system was in place, before she really faced her fears.

I did the same thing with my anxiety. It was a big part of my life for many years, but I pushed it back and refused to face it until I met David. Once I felt his unconditional love and support, it came rushing out like a tidal wave! My panic attacks increased, my avoidances became more severe and my anger surfaced. I didn't know why I was angry; I only knew that I was. Through all of it, David remained loving and supportive.

That night was one of the turning points of my life. I'm not saying that everything shifted for the better the moment I apologized. Quite the contrary. I had scared myself with my own vulnerability and my mind rushed in to try to check my unprecedented behavior. "You're in trouble now," I told myself. "Your anger has always been your power, your strength. And you've given it away. You're allowing yourself to be vulnerable." The voice that I call the subconscious psychologist was arguing on my behalf. "You know you did the right thing. Look how much better you feel. Relieved and proud of yourself." The battle continued. The old, familiar negative thinking that kept me anxious was taking a turn. "You need to keep your guard up. You mustn't soften. You have to appear as though you don't need this person."

I heard the old, defensive familiar words, but it was too late. I had begun a process that, although scary, was somehow cleansing. This was the first time I had ever taken responsibility for my angry feelings. This was the first time I stopped blaming someone else for my pain. This was the beginning of my recovery as an agoraphobic, something I didn't even know that I was. The pure and honest expression of my emotions had poured out, giving me a rush of something new: a feeling of freedom. I was already developing a positive addiction to it and I could not deny it, since I wanted to feel that freedom more often.

RECOVERY IS UP TO YOU

I have observed two types of people who come to the Midwest Center for help. The first type says, "I have a problem and it's my fault." These are the ones we can readily help. In fact, the act of taking full responsibility for their problems already places them on the path to recovery. The other type says, "I have a problem and it's somebody else's fault." With these people, it's much more difficult. Almost anyone can recover from anxiety and agoraphobia, so these people can eventually be helped also, but first, a shift has to occur.

�֎ **We must each claim our own power and recognize our own part in the creation of and recovery from anxiety disorder. In the final analysis, recovery is completely up to each individual.**

Really, this is the good news. My biggest step in taking control of my life was when I finally said to myself, "All right. I'm miserable, scared, anxious, neurotic, depressed, unhappy, dissatisfied, angry, and resentful. And if I want to change any of it, I have to stop blaming somebody else."

Research on people with anxiety disorders has revealed that an extremely high percentage have alcoholic parents or difficult childhoods or dysfunctional families, or were victims of abuse. Any of these circumstances is fertile ground for blame, but blame itself is a fertilizer for low self-esteem. There comes a time in your adult life when you have to say, "Okay, I've been through some difficult stuff, but if I'm not healthy, happy, or successful as an adult, I'm doing it to myself. Maybe I'm holding myself back."

Recognize that the past is the past. You are in control of your present and your future. The past affects you only if you let it.

❊**Responsibility means the ability to respond in a situation with control and calmness. It turns out that taking responsibility, as difficult as it is initially, is the only road to peace.**

When I admitted to causing my own anxiety problems, I had to begin facing the very things I had been running from my whole life. Denial was ending. So was blame. Up until that night, it was so easy to point a finger and say, "This is why I'm anxious. You're the reason I'm so unhappy." I could then feel justified in running away, but I always took me along. Wherever I ended up, there I was, making myself miserable. It was a vicious cycle. I wasted so much time wondering when I would be happy, when I would find peace of mind, when I would like myself or be good enough for myself or for anybody else. Little did I know that I could be free and happy as soon as I gave myself permission to be.

THE WAY OUT

When I decided to be responsible for myself, I began having panic attacks on a daily basis. I was having attacks in the car, at work, and even in the safety of my own home. I definitely got worse before I got better.

My experience is not unique. Many people who have recovered from anxiety, agoraphobia, panic disorder, and even obsessive/compulsive disorder say that when they finally felt safe enough to let go of their resistance, when they accepted their own part in their problems, a lot of pain came rushing out. They actually felt more anxious. Of course this sounds scary, but if the payoff is independence, healthy self-esteem, and freedom from fear, isn't it worth it?

❧ **The only way out is in.**

If you want to take control of your anxiety, you will have to face yourself head on. There are things you can do to soften the process. One of the most important parts of recovery is setting up a solid support system. Make sure that you have a comfortable group of people, close friends or family, who will support your strengths and disempower your weaknesses. This group will prove to be one of the greatest blessings in your life.

One fateful morning, I turned on the television and heard someone talking about agoraphobia. That was the day when my life changed. I automatically began my first positive dialogue with myself, with no understanding that I was using a tool of recovery. "There's a solution to this anxiety problem and I'm going to find it! I'm going to have to do the work. I may even have to research it myself. I have to want to get better, I have to find the answers, and then I have to do it myself."

That was when the work really began. I did the research, did the work, and made the decision to change my life. I had finally accepted an important truth.

❦I couldn't control the world around me. I could only control myself and my reactions to it.

Up until that point, I seemed to be spending time with people who tried to help me justify why I couldn't do the things that I wanted to do. Now, I started looking for different types of people to fill my life, people who would say, "You can be anything you want to be," as opposed to, "You can't do it. It's impossible." I looked for women and men who were positive, more spiritually inclined, with the drive and desire to accomplish great things in life. I found them. They were all around me; they probably always had been, but I had never tried to meet people who supported my strength. In short, I used to have relationships with negative people who didn't believe in themselves and spent their time complaining. I began choosing my friends carefully, spending time with people who were happy and positive, who were going places and doing things to fulfill their lives.

SECONDARY GAINS: EXCUSES, EXCUSES

One of the most challenging questions that people with anxiety problems must ask themselves is: "What am I getting from holding onto my negative behavior?" We touched on this lightly in Chapter 1, a very important concept called "secondary gains." As unpleasant as this may be to explore, we must understand the payoff we're getting by staying anxious.

At the end of one of my seminars, a man came over to speak to me. "The program didn't work too well for me," he said, in front of a remaining two hundred people who hadn't left the room yet.

"What do you mean?" I asked him. "Tell me a little bit about yourself."

"I'm a truck driver and because of my anxiety, I can't drive. My wife bought me this program. She thought it would help, but it didn't. I still can't drive."

"How much do you like being a truck driver?"

"I hate it."

"And how are you making a living?"

"I get disability."

"Why would you want to get over your agoraphobia? Then you'd have to go back to doing something you hate. Of course, it didn't work."

He walked away scratching his head.

When I ask myself what I was gaining from my anxiety, I wasn't sure at the time. It's all crystal clear today. My anxiety was my excuse "not to." Not to change careers, not to take risks. I used anxiety to justify my unhappiness and my weakness. If I got over it, what would I use for my excuses? I would have none. I see now that I was afraid of the shame of failure and I also was afraid of the responsibility of success. If I maintained my excuses not to try, then I wouldn't have to face either of these painful issues.

Many people are afraid to get better because they have become so accustomed to being taken care of. If they managed to become stronger, they would have to give up their caretakers and take care of themselves. They'd rather stay stuck. We are afraid we may lose the one we love if we become too independent, even if our relationship was originally built on insecurity and need.

❧When the pain of anxiety overrides everything else, including the fear of being alone, we realize that we are missing life. That is when we will take charge of our healing.

I suggest that you take a piece of paper and label it, "Positive Things I Am Getting From My Negative Anxiety." Below the title, write down whatever you think your anxiety is giving you. These are your particular secondary gains. Are you getting lots of attention? Is someone else running your errands? Is your fear keeping you from taking risks? Is it helping you to avoid the possibility of failure? Are you using it as a justification to stay in a bad relationship? Is anxiety keeping you from starting a relationship so you won't end up being hurt? Is your anxiety your secret, a perfect way to stop you from being intimate?

Some people think that secondary gains have nothing to do with them. "Ridiculous!" they think. "Of course I want to get better. I just don't know how." If you are one of these people, then this section is particularly for you. I believe that everyone who has problems with anxiety is getting secondary gains. Once you accept this concept, you will understand what you are getting out of staying anxious. You will come to understand that the payoffs that recovery offers are much more appealing than the payoff from using your anxiety as an excuse.

Once I stopped making excuses and I had built up my confidence, I went on to attend college. In the ongoing process to change my life, I was fortunate to find Dr. Phil Fisher, who was assertive, centered, and strong, emanating a mind-boggling self-confidence. From the moment I met him, he became an important person in my support system, and he remains a good friend and colleague. As I watched him function both in his practice and in our groups, I worked at emulating his assertiveness and self-confidence. This became one of my most significant pushes toward complete recovery. We will discuss assertiveness more fully in Chapter 10.

A good doctor or therapist can be a wonderful and useful ally. We have some excellent therapists on our staff along with an affiliate network made up of professionals who specialize in treating anxiety disorders. I simply encourage you to choose a therapist carefully, preferably someone who specializes in anxiety disorders. If you have been in therapy specifically for anxiety disorder for two years or longer and you are not getting better, talk to your doctor and ask for some insight or suggestions. If you feel that you're not making progress, you might look into other options for help.

YOU HOLD THE SOLUTIONS

This book is about transforming panic to power, about fully recovering from all forms of anxiety and emotional discomfort by taking total responsibility right now for wherever you are in your life. You are learning how to be your own sense of security, about regaining your sense of self-esteem and self-confidence. You will begin to feel stronger and more in control. You will conquer your fears and live the life you've always wanted to live.

Whether you view your situation as good or bad, right or wrong, justified or unjustified, until you claim your power and take responsibility for the way you feel, you can't effect a real change or take control of your anxiety.

❄️**There is no magic pill, no magic doctor, no magic anything that will deliver you from the pain. You hold the solutions in your own hands.**

You're going to have to change on the inside: the way you think, the way you react and respond to other people, the way you let things affect you, and finally the way you believe in yourself and your abilities.

Once you are on the road, fully committed to being responsible for yourself and stopping the blame, success is almost certain. I know because I was as anxiety-ridden as anyone could be and I recovered. If I could do it, so can you. You have tremendous potential and now you are gaining the insight and the skills to use it. Believe in yourself! That's where it all starts.

CHAPTER 8

COMPASSIONATE SELF-TALK: YOU HAVE TO BE THE ONE YOU RUN TO

❧ *You are searching for the magic key that will unlock the door to the source of power; and yet you have the key in your own hands, and you may make use of it the moment you learn to control your thoughts.*

—NAPOLEON HILL

Imagine walking into your closet and looking around at your old, worn-out stuff. The sweaters are all stretched out, the business suits are out of style, there is some underwear full of holes lying on the floor and most of your shoes are scuffed up and worn out in the back. Everything seems kind of dingy. "Yuck," you think to yourself, "same old clothes, same old me."

Now imagine grabbing a few of those great big black garbage bags and stuffing them full of everything in your closet. All of it. Empty the entire closet and then give it all away. Now go to the paint store, pick out your favorite color and paint the closet. Maybe a soft yellow or white or peach. Whatever feels clean and new. Get some soft track lighting or a beautiful lamp that gives off a wonderful glow and change the carpeting so that it caresses your bare feet. Good beginning. Clean foundation. Now for the fun stuff. Let's go shopping!

Go out to your favorite department store or to the nearby mall. Let's start in the sportswear department. Pick out some workout clothes in a fresh, light cotton. How about a few different colors? Red, blue, crisp white. They feel soft and fresh, kind of playful. Now let's head over to the shoe department. Buy yourself a pair of brand new white tennis shoes that make you feel bouncy. You put them on and they make you feel energized, like you could run a marathon. Onward to the suit department. Time for a couple of fabulous power suits that will remind you of who you really are. Rich, powerful colors. Navy and black with the perfect accessories. You try them on and they make you feel strong, trim, energetic, and ready to take on the world.

Before you leave, don't forget the lingerie department. As you wander through the luxurious underwear, pick out something soft and sensual that makes you feel sexy. Silk next to your skin. Satin, soft to the touch. Just putting it on makes you want to experiment with it. Maybe tonight.

Time to head back home and put all your new goodies in your freshly painted closet. Now look around. You think to yourself, "Wow, look at all of this. Look at all the potential I see. I'm going to feel more energetic, more powerful and professional, and much sexier. This is the new 'me.' I can't wait to try it all out!" Feels pretty good, doesn't it?

How did you feel when you got rid of all your old worn-out, outdated stuff? Compassionate self-talk will make you feel similarly, even more empowered, confident, relaxed, and sexier. You can accomplish major changes with compassionate self-talk and thought replacement. How do you know when you're doing it right? When you begin to experience pleasure, that's when you're getting it. Don't you want to start now?

NEGATIVE DIALOGUE BEGINS AT THE BEGINNING

From early childhood, we are bombarded with negative messages, especially within highly dysfunctional families. What kinds of messages were you given? Did you hear your parents arguing and complaining about life? Did you and your siblings copy their actions? What about school, where we learned messages like, "Things should be fair," and "If you behave, good things will happen to you." And then there was, "Good things happen to nice people," or "People will treat you the way you treat them." I wish it were that simple!

You defined who you were in your school environment, where you belonged and where you might go next. Did you struggle to fit in? Was it difficult to find your personal style? Unfortunately, very few children and adolescents are given the coping skills needed to pass through these stages gracefully with unconditional self-love and self-confidence.

If you were fortunate enough to be a "genetic celebrity," as we used to call them when I was growing up, naturally beautiful with a perfect body, perfect hair, perfect grades, if you were a star athlete, got the leads in all the plays, and had a "perfect" home environment, then you might have come out of your school years with confidence and a sense of your potential. Some of the most successful people I know, however, were those who didn't come from the ideal background. Since they weren't the most popular or didn't come from an ideal family, they strove to prove themselves as adults.

✤No matter what your background, if you started out with low self-esteem or low self-confidence, it can work for or against you, depending on how you utilize the experiences of your life.

If you're part of the human race, you've been affected by the negative attitudes in your environment and have learned to excel in negative dialogue. Most of us were never exposed to compassionate self-talk; we didn't even know it existed. If our role models had been as masterful at positive dialogue as they were at negative, we would have learned the skill of empowering thought replacement at an early age and possibly have led different lives.

✤It's time to reprogram our minds by changing the negative messages that make us feel bad into positive messages that make us feel good.

WHAT IS COMPASSIONATE SELF-TALK?

Compassionate self-talk is any kind of message or dialogue with yourself or someone else that makes you feel good, strong, happy, confident, relaxed, capable, loving, energetic, peaceful, or motivated. The technique can give you energy when you think you have none, a natural high, and the strength to achieve great things. Positive self-talk can make you feel like running that mile, taking that trip, writing that report, or speaking in front of several hundred people when only ten minutes before you were certain you absolutely couldn't pull it off.

✤The desire and ability to do great things starts with the thought that you can.

These are some of the purposes of learning compassionate self-talk:

- To empower and motivate ourselves and others.
- To calm ourselves in a difficult situation.
- To reassure ourselves when we are feeling anxious or depressed.
- To have compassion for ourselves and our friends.
- To talk to ourselves in ways that reinforce our strength and courage rather than our fear.
- To praise ourselves, to mean it and believe it.
- To talk ourselves out of a panic attack.
- To give ourselves encouragement when we think we've done something wrong.
- To make ourselves feel good.

Compassionate self-talk is the key to recovery, but you can't use the key until you learn how. Imagine someone telling you, "I'll give you ten thousand dollars to sit down at the computer and design a brochure for me in two hours." There would be plenty of motivation, you'd be ready and willing, but if you didn't know how to use a computer, you simply couldn't pull it off. What if I said, "I'm going to France for a month to do some business and I need an interpreter. I'll take you, all expenses paid, and I'll give you $20,000 on top of that if you'll come along and interpret for me." You'd probably have your suitcase packed and be ready to go in twenty-four hours, but if you didn't know how to speak French, you couldn't do it. Could you get up right now and show me a black belt karate move if you'd never studied martial arts? Of course not.

Compassionate self-talk is like any other skill: it must be learned. You have to understand what the skill is, learn the technique, and then practice, practice, practice. Soon it will become second nature to you. When you learn compassionate self-talk, the rewards will be beyond anything you can imagine; it literally will change your life. It will allow you to control your attitude and you'll find a new sense of confidence that will be yours to keep forever.

What Is Negative Self-Talk?

Negative thinking makes you feel bad, sad, angry, helpless, ugly, guilty, overwhelmed, depressed, insecure, and fearful. It leaves you discouraged and tired. Your negative thoughts are a direct cause for lack of inspiration, chronic lethargy, depression, and a feeling of being too drained to even go on trying. If you feel that way sometimes, more than you should, or too much of the time, there is a good chance it's coming from your negative thinking. But don't let it scare you. Instead, imagine your life without it!

The fact is that many people don't know how to recognize their own negative thoughts. Let's do a little experiment. Go out and buy yourself a pocket-size spiral notebook. For the next week, carry it around in your pocket or purse and track your negative thoughts by writing them down in the notebook. Remember to carry it with you at all times. I think you'll be amazed when you see how many negative thoughts you have in any given day, never mind a whole week. Thoughts like, "I'm tired, I don't want to go to work today, it's ugly outside, my head hurts, I feel fat."

You're not alone. Everybody has negative thoughts, even if they don't know it or won't admit it to themselves. You're just getting in touch with the truth about yourself so you can take charge and change.

Empowering Thought Replacement

In order to be a compassionate self-talker, we must learn a technique I call "Empowering Thought Replacement."

Let's read through the following steps and see what we can do to change our old, negative thought patterns.

- **Admit you are a negative thinker.**

If you want to feel better, you'll have to be honest with yourself. Try saying, "I'm a negative thinker and it makes me feel bad and keeps me from my potential. It isn't my fault, nobody's to blame, and I'm the only one who can change it. I really want to become a compassionate thinker and I know it will take some time, so I'm going to work hard at it and maintain it as a goal. It's top priority in my life because I want to feel better."

Remind yourself that it's worth all of your focus and attention. Your negative thinking lies at the very core of your anxiety and panic attacks. When you learn to replace your negativity with compassion, your life will change permanently.

- **Accept your negative thinking as a bad habit that needs to be broken.**

Your negative thoughts are a bad habit, but you've become so accustomed to them, they feel like second nature. They aren't. Feeling bad is not natural and not how we were meant to live our lives. When we can admit to ourselves that we are addicted to these familiar ways of thinking and reacting, we can begin to take the appropriate steps to break the addiction.

- **Be committed to breaking the bad habit of thinking negatively.**

If you want to become an expert in any field, whether it's karate, ballet, speaking Italian, having a successful marriage, or being a compassionate self-talker, it takes a strong commitment. Does carrying around a notebook and writing down your negative thoughts seem like too much trouble? There will be times when you conveniently forget to take it with you or when you just don't feel like thinking about it or making the effort to write down a thought. But you have to do it with absolute conviction and you truly have to want to learn the skill and change your life.

- **Get really good at tracking your negative thoughts.**

When we first started doing group, I suggested, "Let's go around the room and tell some of the negative thoughts we had this week." No one could remember any of them. "All right," I said, "then tell some of the negative thoughts you had today." Guess what? Nobody could remember one negative thought they had all day long. If no one could remember a single negative thought, how could anyone possibly learn to replace those draining thoughts? I told them to get a spiral notebook and write down their negative thoughts during the next seven days.

At our session after they had recorded their negative thoughts, every person came in with pages and pages. It was so effective, they decided to continue writing them down for the next fifteen weeks. In the first few weeks, they got to see the connection between their negative self-talk and their bad moods, their anxiety, their fear, and their worry. The beautiful thing was that as the weeks went by, they became experts at empowering thought replacement. They filled up fewer pages with negative thoughts as they watched their negativity diminish right before their eyes.

- **Replace your negative thoughts with compassionate self-talk.**

You may be asking yourself, "Why do I have to write down my replacement thoughts? It's too much trouble. Can't I just think them?" The answer is no. We must write down our replacement thoughts because we're not very good at thinking of them spontaneously. We have no skills for that. When we write things down and look at them, our thoughts stare back at us. Then we take the time to really think about what we wish to allow into our minds. It's called food for thought, and many experts believe that what we put in our minds is just as important, if not more so, as what we put in our bodies.

Practicing Thought Replacement

The best possible time to replace a thought is the moment you have it. Upon writing it down, immediately write down the replacement thought beside it, even if it doesn't sound right, even if it sounds too contrived or too corny or too opposite to how you feel. It may sound strange, but even if you don't believe the replacement thought, write it down anyway.

For example, here's a negative thought:

"I don't feel good today and I don't want to go to work."

Try replacing it with:

"I feel okay. I'm just tired and I'll get more energy as the day progresses. Once I get started, I'm sure I'll feel better."

Don't worry about doing it perfectly. If you have trouble finding the replacement thought, imagine what your best friend would say to you.

We may not be so good at being compassionate with ourselves, but we are accustomed to giving encouragement to the people we love and to receiving encouragement from the people who love us. You can begin writing your replacement thoughts as if they're coming from someone who cares about you.

❈ **You have to be your own best friend.**

You have to be the one to make yourself feel better. If it seems hard at first, don't get discouraged. Just keep practicing. Everything improves with practice. When the commitment to replace your thoughts is solid, you're well on your way to recovery. That's how important this practice is.

● **Be patient with yourself.**

I cannot stress this enough. The process of thought replacement is so alien to us, it will automatically be met with a sense of resistance and frustration. We've done such a good job hiding those thoughts deep in our subconscious minds, we don't want to bring them to the forefront and admit how negative we really are. We don't want to see ourselves as negative thinkers, but once you see that you are one, you can be just as good at thinking positively.

Begin gently with believable statements. If you wake, look in the mirror and think to yourself, "I feel fat and ugly today," it would be foolish to replace that thought with, "No, I don't. I'm thin and I look just like Raquel Welch." You'll never believe it! Be realistic. How about saying, "I'm going to wear something fun and comfortable today to make me feel good." If you're on your way to work and you tell yourself, "I'm feeling anxious that this is going to be a bad day," don't replace it with, "I'm not anxious, I feel great!" You'll never believe it because it's not true. Try saying, "It's okay to feel a little anxious. It won't hurt me. I'll just relax and it'll pass." That will make you feel better.

Persevere with patience, determination, and kindness. Imagine you are your child and she tells you, "Dad, I don't think anybody likes me." Wouldn't you put your arms around her and fill her full of compassionate thoughts?

Wouldn't you tell her how pretty and lovable she truly is? Do it with yourself and be patient. Give it time to work. When it does, it'll feel great. Most importantly, you're worth it!

THE REWARDS OF COMPASSIONATE DIALOGUE

What if someone had said to you when you were a child, "You can be anything you want to be. You're very special! You're intelligent and creative and you're going to be a unique, wonderful adult because you're already so talented. When you walk into a room, you just sparkle! And you're beautiful, too." If you had been given those messages your whole life, what kind of an adult do you think you'd be today?

It's never too late to grow into the kind of person you'd like to be. Even if nobody taught you to think positively, you can teach it to yourself. You can do this not only for yourself. You can do it for your kids, your husband, your sisters and brothers, your employees, your closest friends, and yes, even your parents. Compassionate self-talk is one of the most valuable gifts we can give to anyone, and it's absolutely free of charge.

How many times did you notice how good a friend looks or how much you liked her new outfit, but you didn't speak up? My husband David is a bicyclist, and I was standing in the kitchen of our farmhouse one morning when he ran in to get a glass of orange juice. There was a hole in his bicycle pants, he had on a worn-out gray T-shirt and his hair was completely messed up. I remember looking at him in his state of disarray and thinking that he looked really cute and sexy, but I didn't tell him. I just thought it. I should have grabbed him, wrapped my arms around him, and said, "Gee, honey, you look really sexy right now!" It would have made his day and it would have made me feel good too. Instead, I just thought about it and he walked out the door with no idea how I felt about him in that moment.

People need praise, approval, and affirmation. Employees would rather stay with a company that gives positive encouragement but pays a little less, than with a company that pays more but gives no signs of approval. I remember a stress seminar I was doing for AT&T in which I was trying to make the point to management about the importance of complimenting their subordinates. To illustrate my point, I walked over to one of the men in the group, sat down beside him and began to compliment him sincerely. I admired his hair, his complexion, his clothing, and then I focused on his beautiful smile. After the first compliment, he broke out in a big grin and wallowed in it. He couldn't help himself; I had made him feel good. The interesting thing is that it made everyone else in the room smile! It was contagious. Everybody wants and needs to know he is appreciated, and everybody wants to see his friends appreciated, too. Especially people with anxiety.

Here are some examples of positive replacement statements that I have found very useful. Try placing these after a few of your negative thoughts and see how it feels. When you get accustomed to the practice, you can add your own to the list.

- It's no big deal.
- I'm not anxious. I'm excited!
- It just doesn't matter.
- I'm okay. I'll be fine.
- It's just my anxiety. I'm going to float with it and it'll go away.
- Go for it!
- I'm taking this too seriously.
- It's not worth getting anxious about.

- It's their problem.
- I'm not going to take that action or comment personally.
- I'll feel better tomorrow.
- Of course I'm anxious because…
- Look how far I've come and the ways I've changed. So what if I still feel anxious?
- So what if…

Here are some examples of negative thoughts. Beneath them are suggestions on how you could incorporate some of the positive thoughts listed above into your empowering thought replacement dialogue.

Negative: When will I ever get over these panic attacks? I feel so insecure and afraid sometimes.

Positive: I'm working on getting over panic attacks. They won't hurt me. I'll just float with these feelings and they'll go away.

Negative: I feel as if my anxiety is controlling my life. I hate these feelings.

Positive: It's just anxiety. It's no big deal. Anxiety is a part of life. I'm doing better and learning to control it. It takes time and patience but I *will* conquer it.

Negative: I don't want to fly today. I feel as if I can't get on that plane. What if I get sick?

Positive: It's okay to feel these feelings. I haven't flown for a long time. I'm not going to be sick. I'm okay and I'm going to be just fine. I'll distract myself and read or talk to someone. It's never as bad as I anticipate it to be.

Negative: Sometimes I feel like I'm never going to get control of my anxiety and fear.

Positive: Look how far I've come and all the ways that I've changed and grown. Imagine where I'll be in six months! I'm really doing well. I'm so proud of myself.

Negative: Why is he mad at me? Did I do something to upset him? Is it something I said?

Positive: I'm taking this much too seriously. It probably has nothing to do with me. If he's mad, it's his concern, not mine.

Negative: What if I have to leave my groceries and run out of the store? I'd be so embarrassed!

Positive: So what if I left my groceries and ran out of the store? No one would care. I could just say I wasn't feeling well. No big deal. It won't happen anyway.

Negative: What if I try the new job and it doesn't work out? I'd feel bad and embarrassed.

Positive: Hey, just trying is an accomplishment! If it doesn't work out, at least I took the chance. That in itself will feel good.

Negative: These spacey feelings make me feel like I'm losing my mind.

Positive: I know what they are and what's causing them. I'm tired today and I didn't eat right. It isn't worth getting anxious about. I'll feel better tomorrow.

How to Be Less Effective and More Effective

When someone is being negative toward you, try saying, "I don't want to talk about that," or "I don't want to hear about it right now." Is this selfish? No! You have a right to feel good. When you've changed your thoughts from negative to positive, you'll begin to choose your friends much more carefully. You'll choose your love relationships more carefully, and you'll choose what you say to yourself and others much more carefully too. What strength it is to choose the messages that come into your head! What a treat to be able to say something complimentary to someone else and make their day!

Compassionate self-talk is the key to overcoming any kind of problem, even when it seems insurmountable. Life provides us with so many challenges; we may be confronted with anxiety, illness, or the loss of a loved one, or marriage, pregnancy, going back to school, or getting a promotion. Whatever their nature, they are still challenges, and when we are in their midst, we require skills to stay balanced. In each and every situation, the ability to talk to yourself in a compassionate way will be your saving grace.

There is nothing more worthy of your time than empowering thought replacement through compassionate self-talk. This skill will make you a better mother, a better wife, a better husband, a better athlete, teacher or employee. Empowering thought replacement will make you an all around better person and will improve the quality of your life. Whether you want to become a speaker, write a book, take a trip to the mountains, get over anxiety disorder or become president of the United States, practicing and perfecting this one skill will motivate and propel you to be compassionate and to have high self-esteem. Instead of thinking negatively, you will be goal-setting. Instead of worrying you will be dreaming. This is how you transform the negative energy of panic into the positive energy of personal power!

CHAPTER 9

THE ATTITUDE OF ACHIEVEMENT:

CULTIVATING SELF-ESTEEM

❦ *The greatest discovery of my generation is that human beings can alter their lives by altering their attitudes of mind.*

—WILLIAM JAMES

Dear Lucinda,

Hello! I am writing to let you know how things have been going for me. I guess because of the environment in which I was raised, the things I had learned up to this time in my life, and the type of personality I was born with, I created negative thought patterns and ineffective coping skills. But at this moment I know I have the choice to change my thoughts and mood for this day, tomorrow, and every other day. No one is responsible for me or my life and happiness except me. I am responsible for my thoughts and the effects thereof, period. This is the greatest and most important thing I have learned from you.

I think that your turning such a negative in your life

(panic disorder) into such a positive is a true testimony of the human spirit, the will to persevere.

Doug

Have you ever wondered how two kids can grow up in the same family, and one brother is successful and happy while the other never finds fulfillment? The answer is simple. It's attitude.

A woman in my group called Marie constantly complained about her brother John. She described him as an egotistical, self-centered kind of guy. She was upset that he lived in a big, sprawling home with a great family while she lived in a tiny one-room apartment all alone.

One evening I bumped into Marie at a social event, which she was attending with her brother. He emanated positive energy; he was remarkably pleasant, gracious and witty. I was surprised for a moment because Marie had described him to be quite different.

They had both grown up in a negative environment. They were only a few years apart in age, and Marie had told me how poor they had been. John obviously had used this negative background as motivation to change his life by working hard and setting goals. His childhood lack and struggles were his motivation to achieve what he wanted and to be a happy adult. Marie, however, had wallowed in negativity, telling herself, "This is the way I was raised; this is the way I'll probably end up."

It reminds me of a saying: "Those who think they can, can. Those who think they can't, won't."

I once took a trip to Seattle with my daughter when she was three. Our plane had been delayed, we arrived late, so I decided to have dinner in the hotel where we were staying. We were both very hungry and it was a long time before the waiter took our order. He wrote it on his pad and then walked away and basically ignored us. He didn't ask me if I wanted something to drink and he didn't bring Brittany any drawing paper or crayons. He just left me there with a hungry, overtired, fidgety child while five, ten and then twenty minutes passed. No food. I finally had to flag down the waiter and ask him for some juice. By this time, Brittany was restless and had begun running around the restaurant.

I finally got the waiter's attention once again by waving wildly at him, motioning for him to come over to the table. "What's going on?" I asked. "We ordered thirty minutes ago and there's no sign of any food."

"We're breaking in a new cook," he said with a slightly annoyed expression on his face, "so everything's coming out late. There's nothing I can do about it." Fifteen to twenty minutes later, our food arrived, burned and cold. We could hardly eat it. The waiter never stopped by to ask how we were doing and when it came time to give him a tip, I couldn't bring myself to do it. I put myself through college waiting on tables and I learned that good service attracts good tips. And vice versa. This man had been so negative and uncaring, he had made our evening more unpleasant and difficult than it already was. My last thought as I left the restaurant was, "I'll never eat here again."

I had a meeting in the morning and we overslept. By the time I got myself and Brittany ready, we had no choice. If we wanted breakfast, we had to go to the same restaurant. I braced myself and walked in, prepared for a bad experience. As soon as we sat down, the sweetest young lady came over to the table. "Hi, I'm your waitress. What a cute little girl," she said smiling at Brittany. "Let me go get you some crayons. And would you like some orange juice?" She returned in a couple of minutes with crayons, two glasses of juice, and a smile. After she took our order, she leaned in toward me and said, "Now you be sure and let me know if you need anything at all. We're breaking in a new chef and he's a little slow." She was back at our table several times with more juice, oohing and aahing over Brittany's crayon drawings.

When the food arrived, the toast was burned, the eggs were rubbery, and the waitress put our plates on the table with an apology. "I'm so sorry," she said. "This chef is not working out too well. Is there anything I can do?" She made jokes and kept on smiling at us. We didn't have a very good breakfast but we felt well taken care of, so before we left the table, I left the waitress a big tip.

The waiter who served us dinner probably goes home at night with empty pockets, falls into bed disgusted, and drops off to sleep thinking, "I hate my job. It's all that chef's fault. He's terrible and he's ruining it for me. I can't possibly make good money there." The waitress, on the other hand, most likely gets home at night tired from a long day, empties her full pockets, and falls into bed thinking, "What a great job! I made a lot of money today, even with the new chef." They both worked under the same circumstances, they both put in the same amount of hours. So how could they come away with completely different experiences? The answer is simple. It's attitude.

You are what you think you are, and it's all about your attitude. If you think you aren't happy, you won't be. If you think you can't be successful, you won't be. If you think you're not attractive, you won't be. If you think you can't achieve what you want in your life, and you say, "What about where I came from?" then my answer is, "So what about where you came from?" Do you want to blame your life on your past or do you want to use it as a motivator? Will you use your childhood as a prison wall to hold you back or as rungs of a ladder that will take you to the top of your potential?

WHAT'S YOUR DREAM?

There comes a time in everyone's life when we have to take charge of our own destiny. When I first moved to Los Angeles, I was recording the Life Without Limits program in a Hollywood studio. I'd get up every morning, get into my minivan and drive through my neighborhood, heading for the freeway that would take me to Hollywood. One morning, a woman in the neighborhood waved and called out, "Where are you going, Lucinda?" I waved back and shouted out the window, "Hollywood!"

"Hollywood?" she yelled back, smiling.

"Yes, Hollywood," I said.

She smiled and shook her head and I drove on.

If someone had told me that I, Lucinda Bassett, a girl who grew up in a brown shingle house at the end of a dead end street in a small midwestern town with an alcoholic father, would end up on her way to a recording session in a Hollywood sound studio, I wouldn't have believed it possible.

So what's your dream? Be really honest with yourself. When you get in touch with what you really want, you'll also get in touch with what's holding you back. Is it your belief system? That's what attitude is: the way your mind works to create or destroy all that you want for yourself. Do you believe you can make your dreams come true or do you believe you can't?

To connect with your personal belief system, take a piece of paper and write down the answers to the following questions:

- Who are you?
- What kind of person are you?
- How far can you go?
- What potential do you have?

- What do you like to do?
- What are your capabilities?
- What talents do you have?
- What would other people say is special about you?

It doesn't matter who you are, how old you are, what you've been through, how long you've had anxiety, where you came from, what nationality you are, or whether or not you have a college degree. What matters is:

✿**If you believe you can, you can.**

When I decided to write my Attacking Anxiety program, I had no idea how to do it. I just knew it was needed, so I sat down and wrote it. Day after day, I wrote from my heart. I already had helped myself, so I knew I could help others. I also knew there were a lot of people who wanted and needed to hear what I had to say, and it came pouring out. I didn't have a Ph.D., but I did it anyway. And it worked! Thousands of people from doctors to teachers, from housewives to corporate salesmen, from unemployed plumbers to psychologists have used these skills to help themselves and others when nothing else worked. The payoff for me is the letters and calls and words of appreciation I receive from people all over the world.

I often ask myself, "What would have happened to all these people if I had allowed my uncertainty or insecurity to stop me from following through?" Ask yourself, "What can I offer the world that I'm not sharing?" There are no guidelines for being a giver. There are no rule books for using your potential. There are many different ways to do it, but first it's helpful to know what your potential is, and then to adopt an attitude of achievement.

ACHIEVEMENT ATTITUDE

It all starts with attitude. When I was in my early twenties, I was driving in a car with my girlfriend Laura. We were in a wealthy section of town, admiring the gorgeous homes all around us. I stopped in front of one that I found particularly beautiful and I said, "Laura, look at that one. I'm going to have a house as beautiful as that someday." I even gave her a time frame.

She sat beside me in amazement. "Lucinda," she said. "I look at that house and say to myself, 'What a fabulous home! I wonder what these people do to afford homes like these.' But never in my wildest dreams does it occur to me that I might end up owning one. In fact, I assume I won't. The difference is, you assume you will!"

When I think about it, what she said is true. I decide what I want to do and commit myself to it completely. I set my attitude to support me in the best possible way. I'm halfway there when I believe that if I want it to happen, it'll happen. That doesn't mean there isn't a little part of me that says, "What if it doesn't happen?" or "Maybe it won't." But the better I get at saying, "It *will* happen," the more sure I feel about it. At this point in my life, there are things about which I have complete conviction and I'm absolutely certain will happen. This is such a powerful feeling. It allows me to approach the various obstacles with a whole different attitude. I look at a challenge and say, "What am I supposed to learn from this?" I once heard that if you want something badly enough and your desire for it remains strong even after you've been challenged time and time again, then you know you're on the right path.

Possibly you're being tested right now to see how badly you really want something.

✽ **The more you practice the attitude of achievement, the more certain you'll become. That's where the magic begins.**

It doesn't matter how many degrees you have, how you look or where you come from. What matters is how much you believe in yourself and how committed you are to achieving what you want. Period. When you're strongly committed and you're clear about what you want, things will begin to happen to bring you closer to your goal.

I Don't Do Depression Well

As my business has grown and I have gone after my personal dreams, I have been knocked down time and again. There are probably more struggles than brass rings. Focusing on the brass ring is what will keep you vital and give you the ability to come through the struggles with a positive attitude. You get knocked down, you pick yourself up and keep trying. Nobody gets everything handed to them; there are no free rides or overnight successes. Some people have developed such a positive attitude and such resilience, they instantly pick themselves up when they're down. I've been knocked down many times in my professional and personal life, and I've found that there are only two choices: stay down or get back up. Perseverance or depression. I've always chosen to pick myself up, brush myself off and try, try again. I've often been quoted as saying, "I don't do depression well."

Whatever you wish to achieve in your life, whether it's having financial success, driving on the highways, or achieving peace of mind and freedom from anxiety, you must get to the point where you believe in yourself. No matter what anybody else says to you or about you, no matter what anybody else tells you is not possible, no matter how many times you find yourself back at square one, you must continue to believe that you can, you are, and you will.

It doesn't get easier when you become more successful. I'm sorry to say that it often gets harder. The survivors are not the people who stay on their feet at all times. They're the Aikido masters, the ones who know how to fall, get up, and try again. They're the resilient ones, the ones who have control, not over what happens, but rather over their attitude about what happens. These are the people who are happy and successful.

Set your sights on exciting goals that are possible to achieve with what you have and who you are. You'll be amazed at how far you can go and how much joy you can experience in your life.

KNOW YOUR DREAMS

Achievement means different things to different people. Success might mean being in a healthy, positive relationship or raising happy, confident children. Fulfillment might mean doing a job that you love, planting a beautiful garden or staying healthy, fit and taking very good care of yourself. For many people challenged by anxiety, achievement simply means being independent and panic-free, being able to control their racing thoughts. No matter how you define success and achievement, you must be clear about what it means to you and what your goals are. You'll find that once you control your anxiety, your goals will change anyway. You'll begin to broaden your horizons and dream bigger dreams. You'll go from a goal of overcoming panic attacks, to a goal of driving distances, to a goal of starting a new job or going on a special trip far away. The potential is continuous and goal-setting becomes an ongoing process.

�֍The ability to define your goals and desires will help
to alleviate your anxiety.

A great deal of ambivalence comes from a lack of clarity
about what we want and a lack of confidence that we can
get it. We tend to blame others for our lack of fulfillment,
when what's really holding us back is our absence of goals
and positive direction. I do a large part of my teaching for
corporations such as AT&T, McDonald's Corp., Chrysler,
Merck Pharmaceuticals, Ford Motor Co., and the list goes
on. In one segment of my seminar, I say, "Pretend that I'm
a magic fairy. When I tap you on the head, your most
desired dream, something you have always wanted to do,
will come true. Maybe you want to go back to school or
have your own store. Do you want to own a cabin on a
lake or a golf course, take ice skating lessons or fly to
Europe? Take a minute or two, focus in on your most
desired dream, and write it down."

The saddest thing happens. A good percentage of the
participants write nothing. They have no dreams. What
happened to them? Where did they go? Have they settled
into a comfort zone where they probably don't even want
to be, and given up their dreams?

When we were younger, we all had dreams. When the
reality of making a living entered our day to day lives,
when we started paying bills, renting apartments, having
families, and taking care of other people, many of us sacri-
ficed our dreams. We gave them up, repressed them or
placed them in the background. These dreams got further
and further away until we forgot they ever existed.

There was a woman who came to the Midwest Center
who was overweight and depressed. She had three kids

and didn't feel good about herself. Not long after she joined group, we did the "What's your dream?" exercise. As a result, she remembered she had always wanted to work in the health care industry, helping people. She started out in a hospital unit making very little money but the rewards came right away. She would come to group each week and tell us about the new skills she was learning. Her depression quickly lifted. Before she knew it, she was doing public speaking and having a wonderful time. When I saw her a year after group was over, she had lost thirty pounds, she was dressing in trendy clothes, she had begun her own consulting business and was doing some traveling. Her attitude had changed, she had gained a new-found respect for herself, and she was making her dreams come true.

ACHIEVE YOUR DREAMS

Have you stopped dreaming? Are you in your sixties, ready to retire, and you don't know what you want to do for the rest of your life? You probably have a good, long life ahead of you, you could live to be a hundred, so what do you want to be when you grow up? Many people have noticed accelerated anxiety after their retirement, because they have too much time on their hands and they can't imagine what to do with it. Maybe you're in your late forties, you always wanted to get a Ph.D. in psychology, but you never did. You had kids to raise. So go back to school. It doesn't matter when you finish or even if you finish at all. Just start. Maybe you're in your twenties or thirties and you think you'll never get what you want because of your upbringing, your finances, or your anxiety. You can always come up with a load of excuses, but I don't want to hear them, you don't want to hear them, and neither does anybody else. Wouldn't you rather drop the excuses and embark upon a plan of action that could bring you happiness, feelings of fulfillment, and help make your dreams come true?

The following suggestions will help put you in touch with your lost dreams:

- **Begin to dream again.**

Instead of talking about not knowing what you want and why you can't do it anyway, let's talk about knowing what you want and how you can achieve it. We start by dreaming again.

If I were your fairy godmother and I could sprinkle fairy dust on you and grant you one wish, what would it be? A cabin in Colorado, a new baby, a fishing trip, a great relationship? Whatever it is, it's your dream. Be your own fairy godmother and let yourself have it.

- **Be specific.**

What does your log cabin look like? How big is it? How many rooms does it have? Exactly where is it? What lake does it sit on? What kind of book do you want to write? Who is your audience? How many chapters will it have? Will it teach something or take people on an exciting adventure? Whose story will it tell? Will it be motivational, adventurous, uplifting, or educational? The choices are all yours. Just be sure that you make one, clearly and specifically. Visualize, make it a reality in your mind, and give it everything you have. Then it's bound to become a reality.

- **Give yourself a time line.**

When could you make this happen? In five years? In fifteen years? Do you hear yourself saying, "I'd really like to go back to school to get my degree, but I have three young kids." First you want to change your "but" to "and." For example: "I'd really like to go back to school and get my degree and I have three kids." Do you see that it already feels more like a possibility? Realistically, could you do it in seven years? How about ten? It doesn't matter. If you're thirty-eight and you could get your degree by forty-eight, that's fine. You're still young enough to have a fulfilling career as a lawyer. Just put a time line on achieving your dream, because without one, it probably won't happen. When you time line your goal, you begin taking action in your life to move you toward that goal, and you begin saying no to things that won't get you there.

- **Make a plan of action.**

What steps do you need to take right now to begin making your dream into a reality? Excuses won't move you toward your goal. Taking action will. If the university is thirty miles away, instead of complaining about how far it sounds, get into your car, drive the distance, look at the courses, and sign up. The sooner you believe in yourself and act accordingly, the more real it all becomes.

If you sit back and say, "I can't do that. It'll never happen," then it won't. The strength of your belief is what creates the end result. Go to a realtor in Colorado and find out the current purchasing prices and which properties are available. Look at the cabins and see what you like best. Go to a bank and discuss the possibilities of financing. If your dream is to start your own business, talk to someone who has already done it. If somebody else can do it, so can you!

- **Take action.**

Do it. Begin with the first step. Remember to surround yourself with people who lift you up, help you fly, and then stand back and watch you soar. Because you will!

How Badly Do You Want It?

When you begin the Plan of Action phase, when you start talking about what you're doing and what you have in mind, some people in your life may try to drag you down and stop you. That's because you've triggered their fear. When they see you stepping out, it makes them question themselves, so they'll tell you it can't be done, that you're being foolish and crazy.

It's easy to believe them because you're probably a little insecure or ambivalent. It's only natural. When I was in the thick of my moving plans, it seemed as if people were coming out of the woodwork to tell me how irresponsible the whole thing was. In fact, it was the opposite. I was being completely responsible for myself, for my happiness, and my success. To fearful people, it didn't look that way.

"Los Angeles?" somebody said. "You must be nuts! Why would you want to move there? Haven't you heard about the earthquakes, riots, fires, mud slides? And I hear the cost of living is impossible! You're being ridiculous!"

All I could say was, "I'm 100 percent sure I'm supposed to move there. These are my goals and this is what I'm going to do." Just because people start lining up outside your front door to tell you that you're wrong, that you're too old or too young, that you're not smart enough or rich enough, don't believe them.

❦**Believe in yourself because you're the only one who knows what's best for you. And you're the only one who'll suffer if you don't follow your dreams.**

I'll never forget when I first flew into Los Angeles. It was 11:30 at night, I was sitting between my mother and my eight-year-old with my three-year-old on my lap. I was looking down at the lights, which were overwhelming considering the small town I had just left in Ohio, population three thousand. My mind was racing. "What have I done? I hope I've made the right decision." Expect a similar experience to mine, but do it anyway. Keep your sights set on your dream. I did, and today I can tell you that moving to Los Angeles was the best thing I've ever done. My heart will always be in Ohio, but the opportunities here have been so wonderful and exciting, if my family and I moved back to the Midwest tomorrow, it all would have been worth it.

WHAT IS HEALTHY SELF-ESTEEM?

When you start making your dreams a reality, that is when a healthy self-esteem comes into play. Self-esteem is directly tied into attitude.

❀You can't have a positive attitude without also having healthy self-esteem.

People with healthy self-esteem believe in themselves. They make better decisions because they trust their instincts, they follow their own judgments, they feel confident, and they like who they are. They share all of themselves including their deepest emotions and weaknesses. They are excited about life, enjoy other people, are happy to get up in the morning, and look forward to life and whatever the day might bring. They know they aren't perfect and that's okay.

When you have low self-esteem, you don't believe in yourself. You're insecure and you almost never feel worthy. People with low self-esteem typically have low energy because they're depressed. They probably don't like the way they look, they're uncomfortable in most social situations, they have few goals if any, because they feel incapable of reaching them. Quiet time scares people with low self-esteem; they often have a difficult time being alone because when they are, they obsess about their lack. Even sitting at red lights can be uncomfortable. They have too much time to think about their fears, their anxieties, their insecurities and inabilities. Then they become anxious. The worst part is that they think their situation will never change. When you're in this negative state of mind, you tend to think that you're a victim, that no one understands you or your suffering.

❊**When you have low self-esteem, you are your own worst enemy. Befriend yourself and take responsibility.**

Here are some ways to begin the process of achieving healthy self-esteem.

- **Recognize that you have low self-esteem.**

Low self-esteem is not a cause for shame. Many of us have it and it's most likely a learned behavior pattern. Simply recognize that you're stuck in a negative pattern and you need to take action to get out of it. Recognize that you can work on your state of mind and change it.

- **Don't let it scare you.**

Self-esteem is workable. Once you have acknowledged your state of mind, if it's negative, let it motivate you for change.

- **Be committed to change.**

Make the decision that you're going to work on yourself to transform your self-esteem into something that will support your growth. Have patience and be as kind to yourself as possible. Know that it will take time, but also that change is completely possible!

- **Take action.**

As with all commitments to growth and change, the first step is to begin. Nothing can happen without forward movement. Step through that wall of anticipatory anxiety! This is a little scary because you are aware that the "old" you doesn't work anymore and is not productive in your quest for recovery. At the same time, you're not exactly sure who you're becoming.

Techniques to Enhance Your Self-Esteem

Once you've recognized your lack of healthy self-esteem and have made the commitment to change it, here's a plan of action. Let the following steps assist you in your journey toward higher self-esteem:

- **Begin by being more positive.**

Use positive self-talk to help you be a more positive and pleasant person. Whenever you catch yourself having a negative thought, transform it. Use your list from the previous chapter. Defeat those negative messages with compassionate self-talk. You have developed skills; use them to stop the negativity and to start cultivating high self-esteem.

- **Treat people differently.**

Instead of looking for the negative qualities in other people, tune in to the positive ones. This will give you a more positive outlook on life. It will make you feel much better about your friends and, ultimately, about yourself. When you're supportive of others, you'll get back the same positive energy you've put out. Then people will want to be around you, which brings us to the next step.

- **Treat yourself differently.**

Making a list of your most wonderful qualities will make you want to be around yourself. Do it and then start telling yourself that this is who you are. If you find this difficult, that's because you're not accustomed to focusing on what's good about you. Try doing it from the perspective of a close friend, someone who loves you. What wonderful things would they say about you?

- **Whenever possible, change what you don't like.**

When you look in the mirror, do you see things you don't like? Are they things that you can change? Have you always wanted a new hair style? What are you waiting for? Go to a salon and get one. Do you wish you were a little bit thinner? Go on a sensible diet and lose those few extra pounds. Go ahead and give it to yourself. You deserve what you've always wanted!

- **Start making decisions.**

As I mentioned earlier in the book, there are no right or wrong decisions. You can eliminate ambivalence by making a decision and sticking to it. Nothing is set in stone. If it doesn't work, you can change your mind, but you have to focus on one direction at a time.

- **Surround yourself with positive influences.**

We are lucky to be living in a time when there are so many positive self-help tools available. Having this kind of access on a daily basis will benefit you greatly. For those of you who suffer with severe anxiety and panic, I strongly suggest our Attacking Anxiety program and our new Life Without Limits program. The Attacking Anxiety program is a step by step audio program for overcoming severe anxiety disorder. It is filled with suggestions from people who have already successfully conquered their anxiety. For those of you who are on the road to recovery and are wondering what do to with the rest of your life, our Life Without Limits audio program does a wonderful job of helping you make decisions, set goals, and take risks.

Try surrounding yourself with positive things: keep positive books at your bedside, put life-affirming statements on the mirror in the bathroom, listen to tapes in your car, and bring small books of positive affirmations to the office to read during your breaks. It'll make you feel good and you'll be systematically and painlessly reprogramming your mind and raising your self-esteem.

- **Start taking risks.**

We will cover this concept more fully in the following chapter, but it's time to start. This is one of the most powerful steps in your plan of action. When you've built a solid foundation for recovering from anxiety disorder, the only way to trust your newfound health is by testing it. So start taking risks, a little bit at a time. You'll be amazed at how much your self-esteem grows each time you take the smallest risk and you succeed. Leave room for mistakes; you can't grow without them. But it won't be long before risk-taking no longer produces anxiety but rather stimulates your excitement.

- **Having faith.**

No foundation can be solid without faith in something greater than yourself. Sometimes, we need to let go and give up control. When we do this, however, we need to know that somebody is there, watching over us and directing our movement for the good of all. I have proven to myself time and again that hanging on will result in chaos; letting go won't. We will discuss this in depth in Chapter 13.

VICTIMS NO MORE

We have become familiar with the skills of compassionate self-talk, empowering thought replacement, and positive attitude. With steady practice, these skills will set you on the road to building your self-esteem, a highly rewarding journey that will allow you to be invulnerable to the negativity around you.

Now you can be someone who is in control of your life and your destiny. The possibilities span out before you to infinity.

CHAPTER 10

HOW TO STOP BEING DISAPPOINTED AND START GETTING WHAT YOU WANT

❧ *My crown is in my heart, not on my head.*
Nor decked with diamonds and Indian stones.
Nor to be seen: My crown is called content;
A crown it is that seldom kings enjoy.

—WILLIAM SHAKESPEARE

Dear Lucinda,

When you told me I would emerge from the cocoon of anxiety a different person, you were right. I didn't believe this at first. I expected to revert back to the old me, but the old me was what got me into this predicament in the first place! When I realized that I did not have to be a superwoman-on-a-string, I think I wept. And (to my surprise) I didn't have to provide constant encouragement and solace to a family member. And I was not morally and legally bound to gather opinions from my peers on my clothes, my loyalty or my skills. Now my words and activities don't always have to abound with perfection and vitality. I have a hearty appetite these days for occasional chaos and gross imperfection.

Now that I am free to be human and to err without thoughts of imminent torture, I wonder how many others will be blessed enough to find their way. The road is long and strewn with obstacles. Sometimes there is no support from family and friends. But even after every roadblock and subsequent detour, I am glad to have traveled those hills and valleys. It is the journey that makes coming back so much more beautiful.

Sophia

So, what *do* you expect? Be honest.

You expect the best from yourself. You want to look good, feel good, and be good at all times. You want to do everything well. You would love it if everyone treated you the way you deserve to be treated, with kindness and respect. You would like all the holidays to be perfect, all your birthdays to be remembered, and all your friends to be trustworthy and supportive. You expect all the people in your life to be honest, sincere, and caring. You expect your parents to be proud of you, your siblings to love you unconditionally, and your children and spouse to understand your pressures. You expect life to be fair. You expect good things to happen to good people and bad people to be punished. Right? Gee, wouldn't that be a perfect world!

Sorry, the world isn't perfect and neither are you. Thank goodness! If you were perfect, no one could stand to be around you. Instead of striving to be perfect, strive to get more comfortable with living in an imperfect world. Strive to live comfortably with imperfection. A great deal of anxiety stems from our expectations of ourselves, of other people, and of the situations in our lives. Let's begin this chapter by finding out how much of your anxiety is being caused by expectations that can't be fulfilled.

Read each of the following statements. Think about how they make you feel. The stronger your feelings about the statement, the higher the number you choose. First find the subtotals for each column. Then add the subtotals together to get your total score. Be honest! Your immediate answer is usually the correct one.

1 = I never feel this way   3 = I frequently feel this way
2 = I occasionally feel this way   4 = I almost always feel this way

		1	2	3	4
1.	I like to be in control at all times.	1	2	3	4
2.	I like things to be fair.	1	2	3	4
3.	I have a hard time saying "no" without feeling guilty.	1	2	3	4
4.	I like things to be perfect.	1	2	3	4
5.	I have high expectations of myself.	1	2	3	4
6.	I worry about what other people think.	1	2	3	4
7.	If I want something done right, I feel I should do it myself.	1	2	3	4
8.	I feel guilty easily.	1	2	3	4
9.	I do not like to fail.	1	2	3	4
10.	I feel that people should listen better.	1	2	3	4
11.	I don't like to cause conflict.	1	2	3	4
12.	People don't appreciate all I do.	1	2	3	4
13.	I'm not where I want to be in life.	1	2	3	4
14.	There is not enough time in my day.	1	2	3	4
15.	I hardly ever feel rested.	1	2	3	4

Subtotal   __   __   __   __
Total of all subtotals   _____

SCORING

0–15   You are a very realistic person. You realize how unrealistic all of the above statements are.

16–25   Your attitude is responsible for a mild amount of anxiety in your life.

26–35   You experience a moderate amount of anxiety as a direct result of your expectations and thoughts. You would be less anxious and more content if you changed the way you think.

36–60   Since most of the statements in this evaluation are perfectionistic and anxiety-producing, you are probably anxious and dissatisfied most of the time. It's your attitude. Learn to let go of this way of thinking.

- If you circled a 3 or 4 on statements 1, 4, 5, 7, and 9, you're a perfectionist.
- If you circled a 3 or 4 on statements 3, 6, 8, 10, 12, and 14, you need to work on being more assertive.
- If you circled a 3 or 4 on statements 2, 5, 7, 9, and 10, you have unrealistic expectations.
- If you circled a 3 or 4 on statements 2, 8, 10, 12, 13, and 15, you have a habit of feeling sorry for yourself and you tend to see yourself as a victim.

Does this inventory help you to see that your unrealistic expectations are causing much of your stress and anxiety? If you scored high, you need to change your expectations of yourself, of others, and of life in general in order to eliminate the anxiety brought on by feelings of disappointment. You've already learned a lot and are well on the way to recovery, but lowering your expectations and learning to live with imperfection is an important step on the path to peace.

ELIMINATING THE "SHOULDS"

All too often, people who suffer from anxiety have unrealistic expectations. You can't possibly be in control of everything at all times so you can't always achieve exactly what you want. Things aren't always fair and nothing is perfect, but people with anxiety disorder usually don't remember that.

So much anxiety is caused by not being able to live up to your own expectations, by feeling that you should be able to do things that are either impossible or unrealistic. It's important to set goals and go after them but sometimes things don't work out, even when you give 100 percent, or when you do everything you were "supposed" to do. When certain things don't happen, we get discouraged. We think life isn't fair and we want to give up.

We are the type of people who like immediate gratification, but the best things in life don't come easily or quickly. Instead of giving up when your expectations aren't immediately met, this is the time to give all you've got! Success is probably just around the corner.

It's time to change your anxiety-producing ways of thinking. Here's a good way to start:

❈Stop "shoulding" on yourself.

Don't let other people "should" on you, either. Many of us have a head full of "shoulds" that are still hanging around from our childhood. You've gathered your "shoulds" in different places along the way, but wherever they originated, they all need to be reexamined and reworded. The point is to decide which ones are yours and which ones aren't. Then you can decide to get rid of the ones that don't serve you or don't reflect your own desires.

Take a piece of paper and make a list of your particular "shoulds." It might read like this:

I should be a better mother.
I should be a better parent.
I should lose weight.
I should be able to handle my anxiety better.
I should be able to handle my stress better.
I should be able to control my emotions better.
I should be able to do this without my antidepressants.
I should be more successful by now.
I should have more money.
I should have more energy.
I should be able to drive that two-hour trip by myself.
I should be able to get on that plane and not feel anxious.

I should, I should, I should. As you look back over your list, think about this: whose "shoulds" are they anyway? For example: "I really should go back to school." Is this your should or does your wife want you to get a degree? "I should lose ten pounds." Do you want this or does your husband want it for you? "I should spend more time with my children." Is this true or is it your guilt talking?

Ask yourself, "Are these things that I want for myself, things I would like to turn into goals, or are they somebody else's demands?" Figure out whose voice is "shoulding" on you and cross off the ones that aren't yours. You'll be amazed at how freeing this can be. Once you've tailored your list to contain only your personal "shoulds," you can use the skills that you are learning in this book to turn them into goals.

From "Shoulds" to Goals

Wouldn't you like to have dreams, strive toward goals, and also be happy with yourself exactly as you are and where you are? It can be this way, but when we are full of "shoulds," we are constantly falling short of our expectations. You can say to yourself, "I'm fine just the way I am and it's my goal to accomplish this." Here's a little trick to help you ease some of the pressure. Try replacing the word "difficult" with the word "challenging."

"The difficult thing about taking this new job is that I have to learn to use a computer."

Change this to:

"The *challenging* thing about taking this new job is that I have to learn to use a computer."

Do you see how this changes the feeling of the statement from something negative into something positive? The word "difficult" suggests a struggle, something negative and draining, if not impossible. The word "challenging" suggests a risk and a payoff, or maybe a goal.

Now replace the word "should" with the words "I'd like to." The word "should" suggests lack. It makes you feel like you're not good enough unless you do things a certain way. The words "I'd like to" suggest a goal and desire without any pressure.

"I should get on a plane and visit my brother in Denver."

Change this to:

"I would like to get on a plane and visit my brother in Denver."

Do you see why it is important to choose your words carefully?

Dissecting Your Expectations of Others

In our subconscious minds, we believe that everybody around us is a direct reflection of who we are. We think that if we have perfect kids or a perfect marriage, it will mean we're perfect. So what happens if our kids act badly or if our marriage falls apart? Deep in our subconscious minds, when we see our children misbehaving or our partners acting unhappy, we are afraid of being judged by our friends. We expect the people in our lives to be perfect, not only for their sake, but also for our own. When we're disappointed in our children for not getting good grades or attending medical school, we think it's about them. The truth is when you dissect your expectations and take them down to the source, it always comes back to you.

ASKING FOR WHAT YOU WANT: THE ART OF BEING ASSERTIVE

Most people can't read minds, and if you want something from someone, it's okay and often necessary to ask for it. Many of us with anxiety don't get what we want in our lives because we're afraid to ask. There are lots of reasons for this:

- We don't want anyone to think we're mean or difficult.
- We don't want to make anybody angry, because they might not like us.
- We don't like to ask for things because we might be denied.

- We don't want to ask for help because we might look weak.
- We don't like to stand up for ourselves or speak up when we're hurt.
- We're people-pleasers, so asking for what we want might not please somebody and we want to be liked at all costs.
- We don't want to experience the feelings of anxiety that come from causing conflict.

A great deal of your anxiety stems from not speaking up when you need to be assertive. You can wear yourself out trying to come up with justifiable excuses for saying no, but we are such people-pleasers and conflict-avoiders that we usually give in. People are accustomed to you being a "pushover," so they'll just keep pushing until you give them what they want.

There was a woman in my group, a sixty-two-year-old grandmother, who was one of the sweetest people I've ever met. Unfortunately, some people seem to think that grandmothers were put on earth for the sole purpose of babysitting. This woman had a hard time saying no to her daughter because she didn't want to alienate her, so she made excuses. Whenever her daughter called for babysitting at a time that didn't work for her, she would start in with, "Well, I really can't because..." and then she would dig herself into a hole with a plethora of excuses. It didn't work; her daughter would counter each excuse with a solution until she got so worn out, she ended up babysitting anyway, feeling resentful and filled with anxiety. She needed some skills so that she could speak up without hurting anyone. Then she could be with her grandchildren when she wanted to be.

You may consider yourself an assertive person. Perhaps you think you're really good at standing up for yourself

because you know how to explode and "really let somebody have it." That's not being assertive. That's being
aggressive. There's a world of difference between the
two.

❊ **Aggressive behavior is hostile and angry; it makes you
seem insecure and out of control. Assertive behavior is
honest and deliberate; it makes you seem confident,
mature, and in control.**

Being assertive is healthy. It's learning to put yourself first
by expressing your feelings and opinions. Sometimes it's
learning to say no. Whatever you need to say, make a clear
statement about how you feel toward a certain subject or
event. Stand up for yourself in a controlled, specific,
mature way. With assertive behavior comes a quiet, confident mind and a peaceful disposition. The more you practice, the better you get and the more comfortable it
becomes.

When people with anxiety find themselves in conflict,
there are a couple of common responses:

- Running away with their tail between their legs. They
  can't stand conflict because they can't deal with somebody not liking them.
- Disagreeing passively, maybe even keeping it to themselves. Or they do the thing they disagree with, just to
  keep the peace.

There is a third, more preferable option, which is just to
say no. People with anxiety know how they feel, they just
don't want to say it. Try speaking up and saying what's
on your mind for one week. Stop apologizing for something you didn't do. Stop doing what you don't want
to do.

Achieving Assertive Behavior

Many people are afraid that when they are assertive, they'll appear selfish or hostile or inconsiderate. If you're using your skills, this couldn't be further from the truth. With presence of mind, we can strategize ways to be assertive with our friends that won't alienate them and will allow us to be kind to ourselves. Here are some steps to take.

- **Have faith in yourself as you analyze the situation.**

Take a ten-second time out. Say to yourself, "What do I want to accomplish by being assertive? What do I need to say to get my point across and how can I say it in 'I' messages? How can I be nonaggressive and still say what I need to say?"

- **Speak up and don't raise your voice.**

Do it as soon as possible. Use your compassionate self-talk. Come from a place of confidence. Watch your posture and watch your eye contact. Stand straight and tall and *just say it!* Use a strong voice but not an angry one. Don't apologize. Keep your sentences short and to the point. Say what you need to say as briefly as you can, then just be quiet.

Question: Can you babysit tomorrow night?
Your answer: No, I can't.
Question: Why not?
Your answer: I have plans.
Question: What are they?
Your answer: Time to myself.
Question: It's too late for me to find a sitter. Can't you please help us out?
Your answer: No. I really can't this time.

Then change the subject.

- **Don't let people manipulate you.**

Don't start making excuses about being assertive or about what you can't do. Don't give someone else an opportunity to pull you back in again. Do whatever you have to do, whether it's saying good-bye, hanging up the phone, or walking out the door.

- **Don't feel guilty.**

Walk away and immediately congratulate yourself for standing up for yourself. When you're not used to being assertive, it's easy to feel guilty and think, "Oh no, did I hurt his feelings? Does he hate me now?" How many times have you tried to please someone you don't even like? How many times have you gone out of your way for someone who doesn't go out of his way for you? Stop it. It's time to start saying no, then let go and get on with your life!

I once hired a man named Elliott to do some remodeling work on my house. He was creative and brilliant, but whenever we made a specific appointment, he would be late or not show up at all. As talented as he was, he was basically irresponsible, and I realized that I wasn't getting any support or a decent return on my money. I obviously needed to terminate the relationship, but I liked him as a person and I didn't want to hurt his feelings. I also didn't want him to dislike me, so I worked up an assertiveness strategy. "When I speak to him," I told myself, "I need to be direct. I need to speak in short sentences and then I need to be quiet and allow him to respond."

That's exactly what I did. I was a little bit nervous, but I said to him, "Elliott, this just isn't working for me. You aren't being responsible. I like you and I think you're a brilliant, creative man, but you're not really there for me."

He tried to manipulate me by being attentive and kind. "You're right," he said. "I haven't been responsible, but things will change."

This was already his second chance and nothing had changed. I had to come right back and tell him, "No, this just isn't going to work." I had been afraid of rejection or that he would get mad and go tell other people I was a "bitch." But the truth was, he was taking advantage of me, not the other way around. Even though I felt shaky inside, I used the steps to assertive behavior. I analyzed the situation, I spoke up without anger in my voice, I didn't allow him to manipulate me, and when it was over, I didn't feel guilty. I knew I had spoken the truth from my heart. The communication was effective. The relationship ended amicably, I hired someone else, and the work got done without causing me any further anxiety. Try it for yourself and you'll see that it works. Don't sit back on the sidelines waiting for someone to make your decisions and give you answers. You can approach anybody about anything. You can solve your own problems.

List of Entitlements

Try this list on for size. It fits pretty well (and it feels soft next to your skin!).

- You have a right to ask for what you need, for attention, reassurance, appreciation, and affirmation.
- You have a right to be told that you are doing a good job, that you are a good employee, a good parent, a good husband or wife, a good lover.
- You have a right to receive compliments.
- You have a right to make mistakes.
- You have a right to say what you are feeling.

- You have a right to your opinion.
- You have a right to stand up for yourself and be taken seriously.
- You have a right to say no without an explanation.
- You have a right to express your anger.
- You have a right to not always be on, feel good, or be sociable.
- You have a right to feel insecure.
- You have a right to feel confident.
- You have a right to question things you don't understand.
- You have a right to be happy.
- You have a right to feel good about yourself.
- You have a right to a good loving relationship and healthy friendships.
- You have a right to pick your own friends, even if they differ from those of your partner.
- You have a right to spend time with your friends.
- You have a right to ask for help from a friend, a minister, or a therapist.
- You have a right to peace of mind.
- You have a right to spend time alone.
- You have a right to rest.
- You have a right to dream.
- You have a right to follow your heart and go after your dreams.
- You have a right to do what's fun for you as long as it doesn't hurt anybody.
- You have a right to feel good physically.
- You have a right to feel sexy, no matter what your body looks like and you have a right to enjoy sex.
- You have a right to feel beautiful.
- You have a right to be smart.
- You have a right to spend time on self-discovery.
- You have a right to seek more spiritual awareness.

- You have a right to play and hav
- You have a right to your emotio

These are only some of the things
to. The truth is:

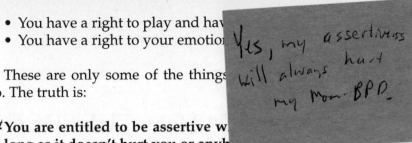

✿ **You are entitled to be assertive w.**
long as it doesn't hurt you or anyb

Start letting yourself know, right now, that you have a
right to recover from anxiety. You have a right to be confident, secure, peaceful, and content. Begin looking for your
entitlements now. Give yourself permission and be
assertive about getting what you want. Remember that
you are special and capable of greatness. With all this new-
found confidence and determination, you can't help succeeding.

CHAPTER 11

HOW TO JUMP OFF THE EDGE AND BE YOUR OWN PARACHUTE

❧ *Far better it is to dare mighty things, to win glorious triumphs, even though checked by failure, than to rank with those poor spirits who neither enjoy much nor suffer much, because they live in the grey twilight that knows neither victory or defeat.*

——THEODORE ROOSEVELT

Dear Lucinda,

I started your program several weeks ago and I must say it has been a godsend for me. I am driving again! Also, I'm shopping whenever I need to now. The weekend of the Super Bowl, we were invited to some friends' house. At first I told my husband I couldn't go. Then he said to me, let's go and whenever you want to leave, we'll leave. After he said that, I went. Guess what? I stayed and enjoyed myself and he was ready to go before I was!

I find it interesting that so many people are noticing the changes in me. Keep up the good work.

Paula

- You have a right to play and have fun.
- You have a right to your emotions.

These are only some of the things that you are entitled to. The truth is:

❧ **You are entitled to be assertive whenever you want, as long as it doesn't hurt you or anybody else.**

Start letting yourself know, right now, that you have a right to recover from anxiety. You have a right to be confident, secure, peaceful, and content. Begin looking for your entitlements now. Give yourself permission and be assertive about getting what you want. Remember that you are special and capable of greatness. With all this new-found confidence and determination, you can't help succeeding.

HOW TO JUMP OFF THE EDGE AND BE YOUR OWN PARACHUTE

❦Far better it is to dare mighty things, to win glorious triumphs, even though checked by failure, than to rank with those poor spirits who neither enjoy much nor suffer much, because they live in the grey twilight that knows neither victory or defeat.

—THEODORE ROOSEVELT

Dear Lucinda,

I started your program several weeks ago and I must say it has been a godsend for me. I am driving again! Also, I'm shopping whenever I need to now. The weekend of the Super Bowl, we were invited to some friends' house. At first I told my husband I couldn't go. Then he said to me, let's go and whenever you want to leave, we'll leave. After he said that, I went. Guess what? I stayed and enjoyed myself and he was ready to go before I was!

I find it interesting that so many people are noticing the changes in me. Keep up the good work.

Paula

Attempting to do the things you fear most often boils down to this simple question: How badly do you want it? How badly do you want to overcome your limitations caused by anxiety? How badly do you want to change your worrying into goal-setting? How badly do you want to control your fears? How badly do you want to feel confident, secure, and in control?

Imagine a scale of one to ten. One means "I don't really want it." Five means "I would really like to have it." Ten means "I absolutely have to have it." Now, thinking about what you really want, take some time—it could be hours, days, or even weeks—to make your "wish list." Sit in a quiet place in your house or go out into the sunshine and ask yourself what you want more than anything. Write it down. Now ask yourself how bad you want it on the scale from one to ten. If you say, "My desire to have this is a three," I suggest you cross it off your list. Since your desire isn't that strong, you probably won't get it. If your desire to have it is a ten, great! You can get it! But first, two things have to change in order for you to turn your desire into a reality:

- Your belief systems must change.
- You must be willing to take a risk.

If your desire is high, seven or above, you are absolutely capable of achieving your goal. Now you must bring your belief system up to a seven to match your desire, or better yet, a ten!

In a recent seminar, I asked the audience to write down one thing they wanted more than anything else. I had time for three people to share their desires so I offered free relaxation tapes to anyone willing to read out loud what he or she had written. One man in his mid-thirties said he wanted peace within himself more than anything. I asked him how badly he wanted it. He said his desire to have it was a ten. I asked him how strong his belief was that he would get it. He said his belief that he would get it was a one. The same was true for the other two people. They wanted different things and their desire was a ten but their belief that they could get what they wanted was a one or a two.

How can you possibly begin to set goals and take chances to get what you want if you do not believe it to be possible? Why bother trying? Why push yourself or take a risk if you don't think it can be done? You must start right now by telling yourself you absolutely can have what you want. You must believe you can achieve your goals. When you begin to believe, you will begin to take action to make these things happen.

What are you proud of that you already have in your life right now? What do you have that you would love to talk about to a friend? Is it your children? How about your career or your relationship? What have you achieved, accomplished, or acquired that you feel good about? Nothing wonderful comes without risk, so think back about what you had to risk to make these things happen. For example, when you enter into a relationship, you risk being hurt or rejected. When you take a new job, you risk being incapable of the work or falling short of someone's expectations. When you have children, you risk giving up your own independence and spontaneity. When you challenge yourself to overcome any personal problem, you risk pain, fear, and feelings of helplessness.

When I review some of my most treasured accomplishments, I see that they all involved risk. We may be creative, intelligent, and sensitive but we are not typically "bungie jumpers." We sometimes have to turn push into shove to get ourselves off the edge and out of our comfort zones to land in the arena of sweet success. We want to wait until we are free of panic, until we are feeling better.

This chapter is about breaking down the boundaries you have put on yourself as a result of your anxious behavior. There are no good reasons for delaying your complete healing. It's time to stop procrastinating and take some risks, because until you do, you will never know the freedom that comes with self-confidence, self-assurance, and healthy self-esteem. It's time to know with complete assurance that you always could have been, you are now, and you always can be your own security!

RESISTANCE PATTERNS

There are many reasons why people don't take risks. Since your resistance behaviors may be keeping you from moving ahead as quickly as you would like, let's take a look at some of them. Once we break them down, we'll have a better understanding of our own particular behavioral patterns.

Resistance Pattern 1: Fear of Change

People with anxiety disorder are most comfortable with routine, even when the routine doesn't feel good and isn't healthy. In order to recover from any debilitating problem, whether it be depression, anxiety, or a bad relationship, you must be willing to change. If you want to gain your self-confidence, your inner strength, and your sense of security, the last thing you want to do is stay the way you are. Unfortunately, change can be anxiety-producing, especially if you're an overreactor and a worrier, as many of us are. But we come to realize that:

❄With anxiety disorder, the only road to recovery is one
of change.

You now know that you have to change the way you
think, the way you act and respond, the way you view the
world and other people, and you have to change your
expectations. Some people resist change by making a decision that they are defeated before they even begin. If you
start thinking, "I know it won't work," then it won't. You
can prove yourself right but you won't overcome your
anxiety. I've heard all the excuses: "The material is too
complicated." "I've already tried this too many times." "I
can't keep my attention on anything." "My husband does-
n't believe in this." "I've have had anxiety problems for too
long and I've heard all this before." None of these excuses
or reasons will help you to accomplish your goal. Let's further break down fear of change into different attitude man-
ifestations.

"That's the Way I Am" Attitude
How many times have you heard someone say, "Well,
that's just the way I am." How many times have you said it
yourself? This attitude is generally followed by statements
like, "I'm the type of person who..." and so on. You may
think you're simply being yourself, but what you're really
saying is, "This is the way I am and I'm not going to
change."

It's not the way you are. It's the mold you're fixed in, the
net you're caught in. When you take this attitude, you're
stuck in a rut and you've resigned yourself to staying
there. Is that what you really want? I don't think so. There
are so many exciting things to try out: new foods to eat,
new dances to dance, new clothing to try, new countries to
explore, and lots of new people to meet, befriend and

maybe even fall in love with. You can be reborn at any time! You deserve this happiness!

Procrastination Attitude

We can come up with a hundred and one reasons why this isn't a good time for just about anything. My answer to that is, "It's now or never!" If you're someone who is still saying, "I'm going to wait and practice my driving when I feel more confident," or "I'll stand in line when my anxiety dissipates," or "I'll socialize when I don't feel nervous around people," then you're missing the point. You need to get out there, get in the car, get in line at the bank, or go to that party tonight. Do it in small increments. Drive down the street and back. Go to the grocery store during off hours when the lines aren't so long. Stay at the party for only a short time and let your host know that you have to leave early.

Although you'll begin to experience little successes, know that you'll also feel anxiety along the way. Expect to have small doses of all of your symptoms, but once you get through them, your skills will take you to a brand new level. You'll be gaining the inner strength that will make it easier and easier to try again or to try something completely new.

Overanalyzing and Intellectualizing Attitude

As we have said before, people with anxiety disorder tend to be overly analytical. Doesn't thinking so much give you a headache? Aren't you ready to stop it? If you don't make a conscious effort to stop the analysis, you'll overload your brain and feel overwhelmed. Trying to figure everything out makes it all seem complicated, confusing, and it produces a tremendous amount of anxiety. Consequently, the old behavior seems easier and getting started or taking risks seems too difficult. This is a subconscious way of resisting.

Try releasing this type of resistance by giving yourself a time limit. Tell yourself, "All right, I'm going to analyze this for two minutes and then I'm going to stop." The mental discipline is essential to stop the pattern. At first, it may be difficult, but it works.

Selfishness and Religious Attitude

Many people feel that putting themselves first would go against their religion. This is sometimes true of certain religions, where we are told that being assertive might be anti-Christian. This couldn't be further from the truth. All good religions are based upon loving your fellow man, and you have to first love yourself before you can love anyone else. Learning to have respect for yourself and loving yourself more will not defy your religion. It will only enhance your commitment to kindness and spirituality of all types.

"Nobody Really Understands Me" Attitude

Do you feel sorry for yourself because nobody understands you? Do you feel like nobody ever had it as bad as you, nobody's life was ever this difficult, or nobody has ever been as anxious as you've been? This is a self-defeating attitude that leaves you feeling alone and hopeless. You aren't alone and things certainly aren't hopeless. I've been working with people with anxiety disorders for over twelve years and believe me, I've seen and heard just about everything. You aren't weird, or different, or incapable of recovery. If you open your mind and your heart, if you trust yourself and your newfound healing process, you'll be amazed at how far you can go.

Resistance Pattern 2: Fear of Failure

We've all been there. We've all been afraid that if we try something new, we may fail. Some of us are already so insecure that if we were to challenge ourselves and fail, we would be even more disappointed in ourselves. That would hurt and we don't want to feel that kind of pain.

Take a minute to think about the "I wish I had" times in your life. What things have you not done because you were afraid to fail? What might be different about your life right now if you had done those things? Would you still have a problem with anxiety?

I remember a man in our group who had an extreme fear of failure. He was a brilliant, highly creative man I'll call Michael. He often complained about his job with a local company. He said the pay was poor and the job wasn't stimulating. Michael was charming and motivating and was quite a speaker; it was a treat to listen to him talk because he had a unique style. I had just become a member of the National Speakers Association and I suggested he do the same. I also suggested that he consider part-time private consulting which could eventually lead to full-time independence.

He liked my suggestions but he was terrified to begin. He was afraid that someone at his company might not like it, he may not be talented enough, and what if he couldn't get clients? Michael just couldn't see how special he was and he couldn't see his own potential.

I saw it. I could listen to him for hours.

The other group members saw it. They loved his anecdotes and stories.

His company saw it. They often asked him to give presentations to his coworkers and he was even doing some of their sales training.

Everyone but Michael saw his uniqueness. His overwhelming fear of failure was holding him back.

I kept in touch with Michael and shortly after group was finished, his company downsized. He either had to take a pay cut and fewer perks or leave the company. You might say he was pushed into changing. Having acquired new-found risk-taking skills in group, he left. Had he not been pushed to make a change and take a risk, his fear of failure might have held him in a job and life situation that never would have fulfilled him. Today Michael is speaking and training. Making more money than he ever thought possible, he is much more confident and happy.

Resistance Pattern 3: Fear of Pain

If you're reading this book and you have not yet gotten in the car, or out on the highway, or gone to the mall, or gotten on the airplane, or gotten up to speak in front of your peers, or made a reservation to visit your family in Chicago, what are you waiting for? One of the things that might be holding you back is fear of the painful symptoms that accompany anxiety.

The truth is, you'll probably have some symptoms. I hate to say it, but the old adage, "No pain, no gain," is usually true in overcoming anxiety. Do not let the fear of pain stop you. You are going to have pain either way, whether you avoid or not, so you might as well be in control and know that the pain is bringing you closer to your goal. You need to get out there, let your heart pound, let yourself perspire, hyperventilate a little bit, feel the panic, but do it anyway. It won't kill you to get out there on the highway with a pounding heart, to feel your body heat up, and to feel a little anxious. You can take it. What you can't take is never knowing the freedom of healthy self-esteem and the release of anxiety.

There was a woman named Claire who went through

one of my groups. After about ten weeks, when she stopped having anxiety attacks, she thought they were completely gone. She started testing it by placing herself in extreme situations that would make her anxious. She actually wanted to have a panic attack to see if she could deal with it and I remember telling her, "Claire, you don't need to test yourself. It will happen, the time will come. Trust me, it might be a month from now, maybe a year from now, when something in your life will test you. The heart palpitations, the dizziness, the feelings of spaceyness and bewilderment, they may come back again and give you an opportunity to use your skills. In the meantime, just keep practicing and getting stronger."

During the week before she graduated from group, she was at her usual bowling league evening and out of the blue, she had a panic attack. Her old routine would have been to tell her friends, "I have to go, I'm feeling sick." This time she stayed there and worked through it by facing the fear and letting herself feel it all, including the fear of losing her mind and embarrassing herself. She stuck it out and used her compassionate self-talk. She reminded herself that it was just anxiety and it wasn't going to hurt her. She got through it and it went away. She proved to herself that:

❦ **In order to free yourself from pain, you must endure it, not run from it.**

Resistance Pattern 4: Fear of Loss

It's common for people who go through our groups to arrive around the tenth week and say, "This is so strange. I know I can't go back to being the person I was because it doesn't work for me any more, but I don't know who I'm turning into. It makes me anxious when I feel like I'm losing the old 'me.' Even though the old 'me' was negative and anxious, at least it was familiar."

I tell them, "Have a little patience and you'll get through this phase."

❦ **It's time to get familiar with the new "you" who is confident, positive, and an inspiration to yourself and everybody around you.**

We all take risks every day. Every time you get into a car, cross a street, or get into an argument, you're taking a risk. You risk in your relationships with your children when you get angry with them, you risk in your relationships with your coworkers when you disagree with them, you risk your health when you smoke cigarettes or drink too much alcohol or eat poorly. So you're a risk-taker. You take risks all day long, but you just don't know it. What I'd like you to think about is this: since you are going to take risks, why not make them productive ones that will help you overcome your anxiety, get you where you want to go, and help make your dreams come true?

Risk-taking can become a positive addiction. Like any addiction, the more you take risks, the better you'll get and the more you'll want to continue doing it. When you take a positive risk, even if you don't succeed, you're still a winner. This can be habit-forming. Let me explain.

❦ **The true prize in risk-taking is the feeling of achievement. It's knowing that whatever the outcome, you have conquered something inside yourself by taking action.**

Once you have felt the rush of conquering your own fear, it will become an addiction. That's where you'll get the strength to go forward and keep trying new things. Things you've always wanted to do. Things you're not certain you can do. Things that, eventually, you absolutely will be able to do.

This is why risk-taking plays such an important part in recovery. When you're willing to take some risks, feel the fear and do it anyway, when you can press forward in spite of body symptoms, insecurity, and fear of loss, that's when you're on the path to freedom and independence.

BEING YOUR OWN PARACHUTE

You can be your own safe person. You can have a sense of security within yourself that you are self-sufficient, that you can take care of yourself emotionally and physically. You can do whatever you want to do and be okay. The bottom line: you can be safe with yourself and for yourself. You can see the world, start a business, and have a great relationship with the inner strength and confidence to care for yourself no matter what life throws at you. It's absolutely within your reach!

At this stage in the process, you've discovered why you have anxiety. You understand the power of compassionate self-talk and how crucial it is to stop overreacting to the events around you. You're aware that you don't have to take yourself too seriously and you don't have to scare yourself. The next step is becoming independent. This is something we all want and now you know you can achieve it.

If you've been absorbing the messages in this book, you're well on the path to being there for yourself. Here is a process to help you establish your own sense of security.

Start Taking Alone Time

It's time to trust yourself and begin doing things alone. For me, this was a big challenge. People with anxiety are uncomfortable being alone because they anticipate and obsess. They worry that they'll lose control and need help or reassurance. They're afraid they'll need someone else to get them to safety.

You have to start doing things alone to achieve independence. How about going to the movies by yourself? Pick a movie that's likely to make you feel good. I wouldn't start with *Dracula*. Try seeing a comedy or a light romantic adventure. I remember the first time I forced myself to have dinner alone in a nice restaurant. I wished David were there with me. I wished anybody were there with me. I was uncomfortable but let me tell you, I really needed to do it. I needed to show myself that I could do it alone and enjoy it.

Time alone is invaluable to staying balanced, but when I was agoraphobic, it was nearly impossible for me to enjoy the simplest relaxation alone. I always had to be doing something productive; I could never sit and do nothing all by myself because it gave me too much time to think. Now I cherish time to myself. I love to walk alone or relax in a bath. I enjoy planting flowers or just sitting outside on a beautiful day, smelling the air and feeling the breeze.

❧ **Even if you know the most wonderful person who makes you feel safe, you really must be there for yourself.**

Solve Your Problems Alone

Are you someone who turns over your problems to someone else? Do you look for others to give you the solutions? Perhaps you're accustomed to picking up the phone and calling your sister, your mother, or your best friend. Whenever anything in my life went wrong or right, I used to call my sister, Donna.

Donna died of cancer two years ago. I never thought she would die; I thought she'd be around for a long time and we'd grow old together. Life has its strange twists and turns. When she died, I had to turn to myself for all that we did for each other. I loved the support I got from her but thank God I had learned to be an independent, secure woman. I handled her death as well as could be expected and now, I'm helping her children find their own sense of security. Both of them have their mother's spunk and energy. Her older daughter Jennifer is in pre-med and is acquiring her own independence. Her younger daughter Lori currently lives with my family and is getting on with her life, trying to establish a feeling of self-reliance and strength. My nieces both lost their most important support person at a very early age, and I'm grateful for the skills that I can pass on as I watch them turn into self-confident young women.

Life is unpredictable and you never know when your safe person or problem-solver may not be there for you. Next time you're faced with a problem, don't grab the phone. Sit down, take out a piece of paper, write down some solutions, and before you know it, you'll have worked it out on your own. Being able to tackle things by yourself is a major step toward self-empowerment.

❊**Working out your own solutions provides you with a sense of freedom and security that is unequaled.**

This doesn't mean you should leave your husband, disregard your friends, or make pivotal family decisions without consulting the other members involved. What it means is that you can do what you must by yourself, you have the answers inside, and it's crucial to your recovery that you know this. You are there for you!

Be Your Own Cheerleader, Toot Your Own Horn

Take every available opportunity to affirm yourself. If all you did was drive to the mall, even if you didn't go in, good for you! If all you did was sit in McDonald's and eat some fries by yourself, great! So what if you only drove two minutes away from your house? You haven't driven for two years, so give yourself a big pat on the back! You did it! You're moving forward, you're trying, you're taking risks. You're learning to get your good feelings from yourself. That's the best part of all!

Now that you've learned to affirm yourself, the next step is to tell other people about your accomplishments. Don't be afraid or ashamed to talk highly about yourself. Take pride in your achievements and let other people share that pride with you.

When I was a child, I had a hard time tooting my own horn. I thought it was bragging and that was bad. As much as I loved my father, it was difficult to tell him about my successes. He was an entertainer, but he never did the things he was capable of doing. Never having felt a sense of achievement, he had extremely low self-esteem and he couldn't support his children in these ways. I remember when I got my photograph in the local newspaper and my father was sarcastic about it. If I shared any of my accomplishments, he found a way to make fun of them. I know now that he was proud of me but he didn't know how to show it. I didn't want to make my father feel bad by reminding him about what he hadn't done in his life, so I didn't share my successes with him.

Luckily, my mother has always loved sharing my accomplishments with me. She's proud of everything I do. I feel the same way with my children. I love to fuss over both of my children and share in their pride. When I've accomplished something, I love to talk with my husband and say, "I did it! I got the deal negotiated." Or "I got the tapes done today and I think they're great!" If I had no one to tell, I don't think anything would be quite as exciting. Success is a lot more fun when you share it with someone.

Now that it's time to take action, let's discuss the best ways to do so, ways that will provide you with the greatest opportunities for success.

- **Be well informed.**

What are your specific goals? What specifically do you want, what are you about to risk, and what are the challenges involved? Write them down and understand exactly what you're facing and where you're going.

- **Be realistic.**

Make realistic challenges with realistic boundaries, time lines, and considerations.

- **Set yourself up to take risks.**

Don't procrastinate. Take the necessary action that will move you toward your goals.

- **Give yourself the best possible chances for success.**

At this stage, it is important to feel in control of the situation and of your comings and goings. Having an excuse or a back door may mean the difference between taking the risk or procrastinating. After a while, you won't need an out.

Be your own parachute. It's the safest way. You don't have to be afraid to free-fall because you'll always be there to catch yourself. Once you learn to be your own security and your own safe person, recovery is in your own hands!

CHAPTER 12

HOW TO KEEP STRESS FROM BECOMING ANXIETY

❦ *We cannot tell what may happen to us in the strange medley of life. But we can decide what happens in us—how we take it, what we do with it—and that is what really counts in the end, how to take the raw stuff of life and make it a thing of worth and beauty—that is the test of living.*

—JOSEPH FORD NEWTON

Stress is the number one killer in our country right now. The majority of Americans aren't dying of natural causes; many are dying from stress-related disease. People come into our clinic and ask us, "Is my anxiety going to kill me?"

We tell them, "No, a panic attack isn't going to kill you, an anxiety attack isn't going to kill you, although recent studies prove that men who experience severe panic attacks are much more likely to suffer a heart attack. The stress response to which you continually subject your body, however, eventually could hurt you."

We can only imagine a stress-free existence; stress is a necessary part of life. The only way to live without it is not to be alive at all. The dictionary defines stress as: "a physical, chemical, or emotional factor that causes bodily or mental tension and may be a factor in disease causation," or "a state of bodily or mental tension resulting from factors that tend to alter an existing equilibrium."

Stress results from negative experiences such as arguments, scary thoughts, depression, exhaustion, divorce, and death. It also can be the by-product of positive experiences such as the birth of a child, going back to school, getting married, or receiving a long-awaited job promotion. Winning the lottery, as magical as it might be, also can cause a certain type of stress. So can environmental factors such as extreme weather conditions, toxic air pollution, and the people around you.

It is important to recognize the stressful contributors to your life. Only then can you eliminate some, minimize others, and change your reaction response to whatever cannot be changed. If you tend to react to anxiety with heart palpitations, dizziness, perspiring, or nervous and spacey feelings, your symptoms of stress will most likely be similar. What you do with the stress in your life will determine whether or not it will turn into anxiety.

THE STRESS RESPONSE: CHOOSING THE "LEFT" BEND IN THE ROAD

Any external situation that causes some sort of emotional response also can cause stress. This is what we call the "stressor." The appearance of the stressor places you at a fork in the road. One direction, I'll call it the left one, leads to anxiety, and the other, which I'll call the right one, doesn't.

When you act negatively to a stressful situation or take the left bend in the road, a chain of reactions is triggered.

Glands that lie just above your kidneys secrete extra adrenal hormones. When these hormones are released into the blood, they prepare your body for action by increasing your blood pressure and heartbeat, making available extra energy. The brain then sends messages through the motor nerves to the muscles in your arms and legs. The internal forces are being prepared for fight or flight.

Back in prehistoric times when we had to run from wild animals, sudden extreme weather, or attacks from neighboring tribes, this was a necessary tool for survival. The speed at which we ran was enough to use up all the extra energy and then some. Today, however, as we sit in a traffic jam with high blood pressure, high blood-sugar levels and a pounding heart, there's nothing for us to do with the energy. We can't fight, we can't run, all we can do is sit there, internalize the adrenaline and get anxious.

Each time you choose to be reactive to stress—and yes, you do choose it—the above response is what happens to your body. Every single time. Then conditions can develop like ulcers, hypertension, backaches, headaches, allergic reactions, asthma, fatigue, insomnia, depression, and the list goes on. In the most extreme cases, when these stress responses have been occurring for years on end, it is believed that they can even result in serious conditions such as different forms of cancer, arteriosclerosis, strokes, and heart disease. Wouldn't it make more sense to choose the right bend in the road instead of the left one?

❧ **All of this is under your control. High stress levels can be avoided.**

No matter how stressful the conditions in your life, you can choose how you react. Since you are smart and creative, you can make choices that will result in healthful conditions.

THE STRESS RESPONSE: CHOOSING THE "RIGHT" BEND IN THE ROAD

When you reach the fork in the road, you can avoid anxiety, sickness, and feelings of pressure by saying, "No. I'm not going there. I'm going the other way. I'm going to choose to be less affected." Take a ten-second time out. Then say to yourself, "What can I do to underreact to this situation? How can I make the outcome less stressful? How can I think differently so I won't ruin my day, or my night, or my week, or my family life, or my health?"

The key, once again, is in changing your attitude. With most stress-producing situations, we have three options.

Eliminate
Modify
Underreact

Imagine you have a job you love, you get paid very well, and you're up for a promotion. But you have a difficult boss. A really difficult boss. What if he owns the company? Let's take a look at your options.

Can you *eliminate* the situation by firing your boss? No. Are you going to quit? No, because it's a great job.

Can you *modify* the situation by transferring to another department? No, because you're about to get a promotion in the department you've been working for several years.

The third choice is the only viable one and it's completely under your control. You can choose to be less affected and to *underreact*.

🌸 **The most successful people I know have gotten there by choosing to underreact to stressful conditions and to keep moving forward.**

"But you don't know my boss," you might be thinking. You're right. I don't know your boss, but I've worked with difficult bosses. I've been in many difficult and stressful situations, and I've seen that I can't control what's happening around me and that I can't control another person. The key is in controlling my own response. Once you get used to underreacting, it will change your life in a positive way and open up your options.

The following is a list of possible warning signals of stress problems. Read through it and take notice of any statements that apply to you.

- Feeling tired. Never really feeling rested.
- Arguing with spouse, family members, and coworkers over minor things.
- Lack of patience. Lack of tolerance of another's incompetence.
- Inability to feel relaxed.
- Constantly feeling under pressure because of job, personal life, or finances.
- Feeling you don't have enough time for yourself.
- Feeling you don't have enough time for your family.
- Lack of desire or time to socialize.
- Absentmindedness. Forgetting things.
- Feeling irritable and tired at the end of the work day.

If you checked two or more of the above statements, chances are good you're not handling stress in your life as well as you could. This chapter will show some of the ways you can catch yourself when you're not at your best, when you are feeling tense or pressured.

STRESS, ANXIETY, AND WHAT YOU EAT

A woman named Helen came to group one night and told us that her parents were arriving from out of town for Easter Sunday weekend. She was having anticipatory anxiety, she was nervous, running around the house trying to clean everything and make it all perfect.

Since they had made the kids Easter baskets, there was lots of chocolate in the house. Helen nibbled on chocolate all day long and by early evening, she was wired up and driving her husband crazy. She had begun overreacting and she felt anxious about what her parents might think of her house. She was ordering her husband around, assigning him chores, and telling him what a slob he was. She also was yelling at the kids for every little toy out of place, desperately trying to keep everything immaculate. Helen was having a stress attack brought on by eating chocolate.

She was already anxious because she was perfectionistic and her parents were coming. She wanted them to think the house, her husband, and her children were perfect. When she started eating chocolate, she was adding fuel to the fire. I'm convinced that no matter how much you learn about compassionate self-talk, expectations, and scary, obsessive thoughts, you won't be in control of your anxiety until you change your diet. You may be diligent in writing down your negative thoughts, in being compassionate with yourself and taking risks, but there's no getting around it:

❀**What you eat affects the way you feel emotionally and physically.**

Some people who are trying to recover from anxiety start out their day with a cup of strong coffee. They eat sugar, smoke cigarettes, eat junk food, and when they end up in a panic attack on the way to work, they wonder why they aren't recovering.

Anxiety and Caffeine

Caffeine is one of the most common substances that will trigger a stress response in your body. Take a look at the following data:

A six-ounce cup of coffee contains 108 milligrams of caffeine.
A six-ounce cup of tea contains 90 milligrams of caffeine.
A twelve-ounce glass of cola contains 60 milligrams of caffeine.
A one-ounce piece of chocolate contains 20 milligrams of caffeine.

Two hundred fifty milligrams of caffeine per day is considered excessive and can result in the following effects: anxiety, nervousness, irritability, diarrhea, irregular heartbeat, inability to concentrate, and an upset stomach. Caffeine elevates the blood cholesterol in your body, reduces iron in your blood, and flushes the water out of your body, causing lethargy and muscle discomfort. Although each person is different, the facts are:

❦**Two hundred fifty milligrams is the amount of caffeine considered excessive, and many people are adversely affected by a much smaller amount.**

Many medications and foods contain caffeine. People who suffer from anxiety disorder can have a panic attack or feel nervous from the caffeine in half a cup of coffee or, from the trace amounts found in certain headache remedies. Read the labels and be aware of what you're ingesting. It could mean the difference between a joyful experience or fighting off another panic attack.

Anxiety and Refined Sugar

According to Dr. Fisher, refined sugar is a major problem for anxious people, children and adults alike. The problem with refined sugar is that it makes the blood sugar levels in the body fluctuate. When your levels drop too low, the body produces insulin and sometimes it overshoots which can result in shaking and trembling. Does this sound familiar? Doesn't it remind you of the symptoms of a panic attack? It feels similar because adrenaline is released in an attempt to raise the blood sugar. Both refined sugar and white flour deplete important B vitamins from your system, once again causing body symptoms similar to those caused by caffeine.

❊**Sugar in any form is not necessary and often contradicts good health.**

Foods that will calm you are: carbohydrates, starches, breads, corn, crackers, pasta, potatoes, rice.

Low fat, high protein breakfasts give you energy. Fatty breakfasts drain you. In the late afternoon, if you get tired or a case of the doldrums, instead of sugar or caffeine, eat some protein. It's also good to know that when you can't get fresh vegetables, frozen ones contain almost as many nutrients. When you eat canned vegetables, be sure to use the liquid in the can, as it will have absorbed many of the vitamins. Do you want to sleep better? Have a banana or some turkey before bed. They are high in tryptophane, an amino acid that aids in sleep. Try a cup of chamomile tea.

Anxiety and Premenstrual Syndrome

Picture a beautiful day in June, the sun is shining, the light is pouring in through the window shades, and you awaken next to your husband. You get up thinking about what a good life you have. Your husband is attentive, the kids are healthy, you have a lovely day ahead of you, and all's right with the world. You walk into the kitchen, pour yourself a cup of coffee, and before you've drunk half of it, you notice that your husband didn't take out the garbage. It's no big deal, they don't pick it up until tomorrow, but for some reason, it starts to annoy you. You sip at your coffee wondering why he can't do what he says he's going to do. Is that asking too much? You remember something he did last week that you didn't like, and you eat a chocolate doughnut and pour yourself a second cup of coffee. When your daughter comes in to say good-bye, her voice sounds whiny and irritating. You get on her case about taking too long to get dressed and she leaves for school upset. Now you're upset with yourself and you decide that another chocolate doughnut would taste really good right now. You deserve it, the morning has already been so irritating. By the time you've finished your donut, you're ready to kick the dog. All he ever does is bark. What a hard life you have! Why does everything have to be so difficult all the time? What happened to your perfect day in paradise? You drank and ate yourself into a PMS attack!

If you're someone who suffers the negative effects of PMS, then you've done everything exactly backwards. Instead of consuming stimulants such as caffeine, sugar, chocolate, and salt—yes salt is a stimulant, causing water retention which you certainly don't need during PMS time—try increasing your intake of magnesium. Vitamin B6, no more than 100 milligrams a day during the ten days prior to your menstrual cycle, could help a lot. Then discontinue the B6 when your period begins. Avoid or minimize alcohol at this time which is known to be a depressant. If you're having a particularly bad PMS cycle and you have a cup of coffee, a jelly doughnut, a chocolate bar, and an afternoon cocktail, you can kiss your peace of mind good-bye.

It is best to avoid junk foods during PMS time or any other stressful time. If you eat chips, chocolate, candy, coffee, coke, cake, cookies when you already feel bad, you definitely will feel worse.

Why is it when we most need to take care of ourselves, we don't? I remember a time before my recovery, before I had any insight about PMS, when my cravings almost got the best of me. David and I were walking through a grocery store. I was cruising ahead of him and with one hand I reached over and picked up a jumbo bag of potato chips. With the other hand I picked up a large bag of chocolate-covered peanuts. Yum! David came up behind me and grabbed the bags from my hands. "Oh no you don't!" he said, as he put them back. "I'm not gonna be subjected to the side-effects of these foods." I was craving salt and candy at the worst possible time for me to be eating it!

❈**During a PMS cycle, your body is already fighting a great deal of stress. When you add the adrenaline that the intake of junk foods will produce, you'll feel ten times worse.**

Don't do it to yourself. Think first. Take a ten-second time out. Then, make yourself a nice hot cup of chamomile tea and keep yourself calm.

Nervous Stomach

Many people with anxiety disorder complain of nervous stomach or diarrhea. Irritable Bowel Syndrome, which is a combination of cramping, diarrhea, and constipation, was a real problem for me. It is common to many people with anxiety disorder. For starters, eliminating caffeine and alcohol from your diet will be extremely helpful. If you suffer with constant diarrhea and cramping, I strongly suggest you see your doctor and begin to change your diet. Unless you suffer with severe disorders of the bowel, you would benefit from eating two tablespoons of raw, unprocessed bran daily, but it often causes gas at first. If you suffer from chronic constipation, see your doctor. Eating bran regularly will usually solve both constipation and diarrhea by regulating your system. Since it is very filling, eating bran possibly will help you to eat less food.

Drink an eight-ounce glass of water with the bran. Eating bran will regulate your bowels and minimize your chances of colon cancer. It tastes best in cereal or yogurt.

Summary of Diet and Nutrition

Keep in mind the following points about nutrition to stay within a healthy food program. It will benefit you more than you can imagine: you'll feel better, you'll have more energy, less anxiety, you'll be less irritable, and people will find you much more fun to be around.

- Start now to minimize sweets in your diet. You might find this hard at first because the more you eat sugar the more you crave it. Give yourself a few weeks to break the addiction. Eventually the craving will dissipate. Guaranteed to cause anxiety, panic feelings, and irritability—cookies, candy, chocolate and all sugars should be avoided.
- Eat more fruits and raw vegetables. It is believed that five fruits and vegetables a day can help prevent cancer. They are great source of fiber. Remember frozen

vegetables are more nutritious than canned, and when eating canned vegetables be sure to drink the juice which is full of nutrients.

- Include raw bran in your diet daily. It will help regulate your bowels and help control your appetite. Choose whole wheat grains in breads and cereals.
- Minimize your consumption of fatty foods such as hot dogs, sausage, bakery goods, butter, and cheese. Fat doesn't digest well and makes you feel tired. Eating fatty foods contributes to serious health problems such as heart disease, obesity, and cancer.
- Eat more fish and chicken. Broil it and remove the skin from chicken, which contains most of the fat.
- Use less salt. It causes water retention and can add to symptoms of anxiety. Experiment with other spices.
- Drink as much water as you possibly can on a daily basis. It cleanses the system and aids in overall good health.
- Eat light meals, especially before bedtime. Always sit down, eat slowly, and enjoy your food.
- Avoid caffeine! It will make you anxious and irritable and increase your blood sugar. If you are currently drinking caffeine on a regular basis, you will have to cut down gradually. Expect irritability and headaches initially. Once you eliminate it, you will be amazed at how much less anxious you feel.
- Minimize your alcohol consumption. Alcohol will make you feel depressed and tired. It disrupts healthy sleep patterns and is a health risk. Many people complain of increased feelings of anxiety the day after a night of drinking alcohol.

The local health food store is a great resource for alternative choices for natural products that will give you energy and make you feel relaxed. Many herbs, teas, and vitamin products can do more to energize or relax you than caffeine or a glass of wine, and there are no detrimental side effects.

ANXIETY AND TIME MANAGEMENT

People with anxiety tend to push themselves too hard. They often overload their schedules, trying to get too much done in a limited amount of time. They race against the clock, exhausted and irritable, turning their stress into anxiety. Some people with anxiety disorder are always rushing. They drive fast, talk fast, eat fast, they pack three days into one, and at the end of the day, they never feel that they've done enough. They have little tolerance for others who speak slowly or take their time getting places. In other words, they are impatient.

As you begin to acquire coping skills, stop and ask yourself some important questions: What's the rush? What's so all-fired important? Where am I going and where will I be when I get there? Is it a matter of life and death? Am I rushing through my days and rushing through my life? Am I missing the present moment? Am I always in a hurry and do I always feel that there isn't enough time?

Guess what?

❧**We all have 24 hours in our day. We choose how to use them.**

Don't say that you don't have time to read a book. Say you're not giving yourself time to read the book. Don't say that you don't have time to exercise. Say you're not taking the time to exercise. Since you decide what to do with your time, you can start making different choices. There's time to do what's important for you. And time to do nothing is just as important as being productive.

When you push too hard, guess what happens? You get to spend time with your old friend, Body Symptoms. It's time to start taking care of yourself. Try saying, "All right. I'm having anxiety symptoms. That means I'm stressed out so I'll finish this report tomorrow. I'll clean the house another time. There's no food in the house and I have no time to go to the store. I'll order take-out." That's being responsible. That's managing your time to eliminate anxiety. That's being compassionate with yourself.

Don't Just Do Something, Sit There!

Sometimes, doing nothing is the healthiest decision, but believe me, it takes practice. Especially for someone prone to anxiety. You're so used to running and doing and accomplishing. Deep down inside, wouldn't you rather sit back, put your feet up, read a book, take a bath or a nap, and stop everything?

People with anxiety are afraid to have time to think, time to do nothing, time to be alone, time to just be. Those of us with anxiety disorder subconsciously are afraid of having time on our hands.

Being Efficient

When you visualize an efficient person, what do you see? Is it a secretary sitting at her desk, busy, busy all the time, sweat pouring off her brow, putting out tremendous effort and large amounts of finished work? That's not efficient. That's somebody with high anxiety and lots of pressure.

❀ **The true meaning of efficient is getting the most done with the least amount of effort.**

To be a truly efficient person, work out when you function best during the day. Everybody has a peak productivity period. If you're a morning person, schedule your demanding tasks in the morning. This is when you could do your accounting, give your presentation, have that confrontation. If you tend to drag in the midafternoon, plan a rest period where you put your feet up and have some herbal tea and a healthy snack. You could use that time to answer calls instead of spending your most productive morning time on the phone. Your low energy period is probably when some of your best creative work will come pouring out, so write in your journal. Knowing your peak energy times and low energy times will help you to plan a more relaxed and productive day.

Learning to say no is another important aspect of time management. Take on what you want to do or what's absolutely necessary and say no to the rest. You don't have to make excuses for not doing something. Your time belongs to you, not to anybody else.

Guidelines to Managing Energy

Time is not a hand on a clock that races ahead of you no matter how fast you go. If you look at it as an enemy, you'll experience it that way. It's all about attitude. The truth is that time is nothing more than energy.

❈**When you waste time, you waste energy. When you manage your energy, you also manage and time.**

Here are some important ways to control the amount of energy you use in a day. As you follow these guidelines, you'll be learning to stop your stress from becoming anxiety:

- Take a look at what you need to do at the beginning of the day or the end of the previous day. What can you eliminate or delegate to someone else?
- Break down the day into segments. Choose the order in which to do the most important errands. Don't begin one until you've completed the last, unless doing them together would be more efficient.
- Don't overload your day; underload it. Then, if you have extra time and energy, you can add something to the list.
- Take a break during the day. Relax, think positively, and do something pleasant like having a healthy snack or taking a short walk.
- Adopt a relaxed attitude toward time. Nothing is all that important in the scheme of things. Try to avoid feeling rushed and pressured, especially when you're working, driving, or running errands. Slow down and enjoy your time.
- Listen to your body signals. When you feel tired, stop. If you're beginning to have symptoms, it's because you're pressured. Use your skills to relieve the stress.
- Avoid irritating, negative people whenever possible. If not possible, don't let them "get to you." Underreact.
- Avoid caffeine and sugar.
- Spend time alone at the end of each day to relax, read, or listen to tapes. If you want it badly enough, you can take half an hour for yourself.
- Learn to say no to other people's demands on your time. You'll feel guilty at first, but eventually you'll feel a wonderful sense of freedom and self-control.
- If you have to push yourself, plan ahead and do it in a way that will demand the least from you. With a relaxed attitude, the day will come off more relaxed.
- Slow down. Talk, walk, and do everything more

slowly and in a more relaxed way. You'll be amazed at how much more in control you feel and how much more you'll accomplish.

- Keep it simple. What can you do to simplify your life? What simple pleasures can you focus upon? Simplify, simplify, simplify.

Finally, remember to stop and smell the roses. Look around. The most wonderful things in life aren't about stress and pressure. They are warm and beautiful and free: a spectacular sunset, the smell of fresh flowers, the feel of soft grass beneath your bare feet. A warm caress from your child or friend. A good laugh. A good book and a warm blanket. These are the things that make up a peaceful life. Keep it simple.

CHAPTER 13

TO MEDICATE OR NOT TO MEDICATE: THAT IS THE QUESTION

Dear Lucinda,

You know I am writing to someone I have never met but who seems like a life long friend. I met you on my 47th birthday. Your program was given to me by my wife.

So, today I graduated from the course. I now have control over me, for the first time in so many years. I have reduced my Ativan to .5 mg per day! I am very proud of this. I was addicted for so long. I took them for headaches, toothaches, everything! It no longer controls me, now it is just a tool until I reach the correct time to eliminate it.

I wish you knew how much I have changed! I am a new person. My wife cannot get over the change and neither can I. I go shopping, take my wife to breakfast, go to work with minimum of meds, and so on. I did not do some of these things without anxiety, or didn't do them at all before.

So Lucinda this is to say Thank You for helping me

change my life. I am going to keep growing and learning. I am in control and I love it!

Frederick

Throughout this book, we have seen that different people have different needs. If you are presently on medication for anxiety and depression, don't feel badly about it. Your need for medication doesn't mean that you're weak or dependent or weird or crazy. Taking medication doesn't mean that you're hopeless or helpless or ultimately unable to cope in the real world. It doesn't mean that you'll be on medication for the rest of your life. Anxiety and depression are treatable.

When you change your thoughts, you also change your brain chemistry. You can be your own chemist and change your internal brain chemistry for the better just by thinking differently. When you learn how to underreact, respond differently, use compassionate self-talk, and be more assertive, you actually create more endorphins and reduce your catecholamine activity.

When you reach out to hug your wife or to give her a great big heartfelt kiss, you cause a chemical reaction in your own brain. In fact, just about everything we do causes a chemical reaction: when we eat, when we laugh, when we cry, when we speak, when we dance, when we fall asleep. Any kind of activity creates a chemical response in the brain which triggers a reaction in the body. So don't let the words "biochemical response" scare you.

This doesn't mean you shouldn't use medication. It doesn't mean that if you're too anxious to drive your car or give a talk in front of people or get on a plane, that you shouldn't be on some sort of medication for a short while until you acquire some skills. It means that chemical reactions are happening in all of us all of the time. What we do about them is another story because there are many different options, and as we said in the opening of this chapter different people have different needs.

ANTI-ANXIETY MEDICATION: THE PROS AND CONS

A woman once came into one of my groups who had had severe anxiety disorder for many years. Her doctor had told her that she would have to be on anti-anxiety medication for the rest of her life and she was quite upset about that. She had never liked medications, she was afraid of the side-effects and the addiction potential, but she was literally nonfunctional without her medication. She was on both anti-anxiety medication and an antidepressant. She had never learned any effective coping skills and her doctor had never even told her there were such things.

After going through the Attacking Anxiety program and practicing the various techniques and exercises, she slowly reduced her medication. Six months after joining group, she was medication-free. If your doctor has told you that you will be on anti-anxiety medication for life, you might want to find a different doctor, one that understands that there are options and coping skills that can help you become medication free.

IMPORTANT NOTICE: If you are on medication, you must seek the advice of your doctor before you decide to cut down. It is important to decrease most medications gradually and only with your doctor's guidance.

The most often prescribed medications for anxiety are benzodiazepines, which in some cases have proven to be quite effective. Since there is potential for addiction, these drugs are generally prescribed for limited periods of time in limited dosages. Preferably they are used as part of an overall treatment program which hopefully includes coping skills and behavior modification techniques.

The most common drugs prescribed for anxiety symptoms are the benzodiazepines Xanax (alprozalam) and Klonopin (cloazepam). Ativan and Tranxene are also prescribed. All are potentially habit-forming. This is of special concern to anyone who has had or still has a drug or alcohol addiction. Valium (diazepam) used to be prescribed for anxiety, but more and more physicians are realizing that there are better medications from which to choose. A newer medication called Busiprone appears to be non-habit-forming, and so far has been shown to have fewer side-effects than some of the other anti-anxiety medications. Again, if the decision is made to use anti-anxiety medication, it is preferable that it be used in small doses over a short period of time while you are learning various coping skills.

A man came into group one week to tell us that for the first time, while he was at a gathering, he had left his medication in his pocket and forgotten to take it. It was not long before he had stopped it altogether, with the guidance of his doctor. This is typical of someone who is working diligently with the program. You gradually decrease your medication and the need for it often falls away organically.

DEPRESSION

Different people have told me a variation of this idea: "I just don't know what's wrong with me. I don't have panic attacks any more, I have my anxiety under control, but I don't feel happy. What's wrong with me?"

Depression might be what's wrong. We believe that depression accompanies anxiety in approximately 85 percent of the cases. Although depression often heals itself in the long run, some people can't wait until the long run. In some cases, no amount of coping skills, techniques, or exercises will eliminate depression fast enough. Antidepressant medication can be extremely helpful in a fairly short period of time and doesn't seem to have the potential for addiction that many anti-anxiety medications do.

Depression seems scary. I've seen people at the Midwest Center who are more than willing to discuss all aspects of their anxiety, but they have a difficult time accepting the fact that they might be depressed. They see it as a failure, a lack, or a deficiency, something worthy of shame or fear. It isn't any of these things. People can't help being depressed any more than they can help having diabetes. If your doctor said you had diabetes, would you be ashamed to take insulin? If you had a thyroid problem, would you be embarrassed to tell someone you took thyroid medication? These are medical conditions just like depression. The good news is that depression can often be helped by coping skills like the ones you are learning in this book.

If you learn these skills, if you take action to control your anxiety and your life, and you still feel the following symptoms, I strongly suggest you talk with your doctor about depression.

Symptoms of depression include but are not limited to:

- Feeling tired often
- Lack of enthusiasm about the future
- Lack of enthusiasm about life in general
- Extreme sadness
- Crying often for seemingly no reason
- Loss of appetite
- Overeating
- Headaches
- Uncontrollable emotions
- Aches and pains

- Sleeping too much
- Insomnia
- Waking in the night
- Feelings of hopelessness
- Feeling that there is no help for you
- Feelings of inadequacy
- Suicidal thoughts

When you are experiencing severe depression, including feelings of complete hopelessness and thoughts of suicide, you need help. It's common for people with anxiety to have suicidal thoughts, because the anxiety scares them so much that they think they can't live with it. But they aren't actually suicidal. People who are truly suicidal aren't frightened by their thoughts. For them, suicide seems as if it would be a relief and the thought is more comforting than frightening.

❦IF YOU ARE AT THE POINT WHERE YOUR SUICI-DAL THOUGHTS COMFORT YOU, CALL YOUR DOCTOR IMMEDIATELY.

With this kind of depression you feel like you fell into a black hole, that there isn't any hope and you'll never come out of it. That isn't true, it's merely a part of the illness, but when you feel that down, call for help and don't waste time.

Other Types of Depressive Conditions

A gorgeous professional woman once came into the Midwest Center and told us about going on spending sprees when she spends hundreds, even thousands of dollars she doesn't have. She was a manic-depressive and in the manic swing of her disorder, she would go binge shopping. When she hit the depressive side, however, she lost all interest in doing anything at all. She became depressed, she cried a lot, and she didn't want to get out of bed. She had severe suicidal thoughts. These extreme highs and lows are typical of manic-depression. When you're high, you may have massive amounts of creative energy and you might think you can do anything from starting a new million-dollar business to flying to a foreign country on a whim. You may spend money you don't have and you hardly sleep. When you're low, the whole world looks bleak and alien. You lose your appetite, you sleep too much, and you feel suicidal. Manic-depression requires a doctor's help and medication.

There are medications that have proven effective, and many manic-depressive people are leading normal lives. The problems occur when manic-depression is misdiagnosed and people are put on the wrong medications. This can actually increase the symptoms, so make sure your doctor is well trained in both anxiety and depression.

Another type of depression is called bipolar disorder, which is characterized by mood swings. One day you're up, feeling good, and the next day you're down, feeling tired and depressed. Again, there are various medications that can be extremely helpful in treating bipolar disorder. Consult with your doctor.

❀ There are certain medications that work for each of these depressive disorders and it's important to get accurately diagnosed.

Then you can work with your doctor and find the correct medication and dosage that will allow you to feel good and have a peaceful life. We all deserve it and it is truly possible for everyone.

Antidepressant Medications

In many mild to severe cases, antidepressant medications can be very helpful. These drugs don't make you happy and they don't make you high. If you feel that you've gotten a grip on your anxiety but can't seem to get anywhere with your depression, don't be afraid to try a mild antidepressant medication.

They are usually given in gradually increasing dosages until an effect is apparent. It may be necessary for your doctor to have you try out several different types before you find the one that works best for you. The most often prescribed drugs have been the tricyclics, such as Asendin, Elavil, Norpramin, Pamelor, Sinequan, and Tofranil. Side-effects might include drowsiness, slight dizziness, dry mouth, constipation, and a change in urinary habits. Fortunately, some of the side-effects disappear in several weeks. Some types of antidepressants can help to suppress panic attacks. Prozac and Zoloft are quite popular these days, as they seem to be effective not only in treating depression and symptoms of panic, but in controlling obsessive thoughts as well. Prozac has also proven helpful for women with symptoms of premenstrual syndrome. Talk with your doctor.

I would rather see someone on a mild antidepressant than on an anti-anxiety medication, because they are not habit-forming and won't cause detrimental side-effects over a long period of time. Antidepressants can take the edge off a little bit and they can calm you down and help you feel balanced. It may take up to four weeks to feel the benefits of these medications, so patience and an understanding of side-effects is important. When it comes to making decisions about medication, the bottom line is that you must be well informed.

❦ **Talk to your doctor, read all the available literature, know what you're taking, and be aware of all possible side-effects.**

Perhaps you want to learn your coping skills, be patient and see if you can do it without any medication. I certainly encourage you to do so. If you finally decide to take medication, do it from a clear place and be well informed. Check with your doctor and let him or her determine if you are a candidate for medication. Just remember that whatever your choice, you needn't judge yourself, you needn't feel shame or a sense of failure. Whether you medicate or not, you have the same goal: complete recovery from anxiety and feelings of depression.

SELF-MEDICATING WITH ALCOHOL

Some people cannot tolerate medication of any kind. Are you someone whose system is just too sensitive to handle it? If you are, alcohol is not the answer. If you have a genetic background that is prone to anxiety, depression, and/or alcoholism, a couple of glasses of chardonnay in the evening to help you relax would be a detrimental way to go. Light social drinking is one thing, but if you can't sleep without a few glasses of wine, if you can't relax and mingle at a party without a few drinks, you need to take a good look at yourself. This is true particularly if you're taking medication, as the combination of drugs and alcohol is most often damaging and could be deadly.

Dr. Fisher believes that if you're having three or more alcoholic beverages a day, you probably have an alcohol addiction, but it's different for everyone. I personally feel that daily alcohol consumption might be a need for concern. It seems there is a chemical site in our brain at which point alcohol interacts in an addictive fashion. Some people with anxiety have a tendency to use it to self-medicate because it seems to relieve the body symptoms. In the long run, however, it will become a serious addiction and it will make you feel worse and worse as time goes on.

Sometimes it's difficult to determine whether or not you have a drinking problem. Take the following inventory and see where you stand.

- When you are in crisis or feel under pressure, do you drink more than usual?
- Have you noticed that you can handle more alcohol now than when you first started drinking?
- Do you ever wake up "the morning after" and discover that you can't remember things about the previous night?
- When drinking with others, do you try to have a few extra drinks while nobody's watching?
- Are there occasions when you feel uncomfortable if alcohol isn't available?
- Are you in more of a hurry to have the first drink now, than when you began drinking?
- Do you feel guilty about your drinking?
- Have you ever felt annoyed by criticism of your drinking?
- Have you ever felt the need to cut down on your drinking?
- Have you ever taken a morning "eye-opener"?
- Do you drink alcohol every day?

If you answered "yes" to two or more of these questions, you might have a drinking problem. The more "yes" answers you have, the more severe your problem.

If you've discovered that you're self-medicating with alcohol, you need to be honest with yourself. Perhaps you're trying to take the edge off and perhaps that edge is anxiety. If you face reality and have some compassion for yourself, you can feel better and get rid of your addiction. You can learn to live a good life and find peace with little or no alcohol.

What Are We Reaching For?

There is a yearning inside each of us, a yearning for something better, for something more. We're all reaching for peacefulness and fulfillment. We want to feel happy and connected. We can.

We must give ourselves permission to be free, for freedom begins inside of us. Let's read on and explore what lies at the foundation of a peaceful life.

CHAPTER 14

LEAP OF FAITH: FREE AT LAST!

❖ *For all his learning or sophistication, man still instinctively reaches toward that force beyond… Only arrogance can deny its existence, and the denial falters in the face of evidence on every hand, in every tuft of grass, in every bird, in every opening bud, there it is.*

—HAL BORLAND

My friend Jackie is one of the dearest souls I've ever known. She worked with me for many years and when I think of someone who is the embodiment of a loving and unselfish human being, it's Jackie.

Four or five years ago Jackie started feeling poorly, passing out and having some other severe symptoms. When she went to the doctor, our worst fears were realized. She was diagnosed with a rare form of cancer. Five years later, she's a medical miracle. Only this year has she had to take medication and undergo treatments. She's breaking all the rules, defying all the statistics, and she's having a great life. I know how she has achieved all of this: it's her attitude of unconditional faith and trust.

A short time ago when I was in Ohio on a business trip, I went to visit Jackie. I was sitting beside her on the couch when suddenly she reached up to the wall beside us, took down a picture of two baby sea lions, and placed it in my hands. I looked closely at these innocent, playful creatures lying all over each other and then I saw the words "Fragile Trust" written across the bottom.

"Look at the title," Jackie said. "'Fragile Trust.' Isn't that beautiful?"

"This is what Jackie is and what she stands for," I thought to myself. "A gentle creature with a trust so beautiful and an open heart so fragile, it makes mine want to reach out to her." Jackie was and still is the epitome of trust. Her mind and her heart are warm and open, and she keeps on trusting everyone, her friends, her doctors, and above all, God. No matter how much pain she is going through, no matter the severity of the diagnosis.

"How are you doing?" I often ask her.

"I'm doing well," she'll answer.

She means it. She might be in terrible pain that day, she might have lost sleep or lost her appetite but she never loses her faith. She believes with all her heart that she is going to be okay. She believes with all her soul that she has total support and love around her. That's why she's telling the truth when she says she's doing well. She doesn't focus on her illness; she focuses on living in the present.

Some people may think she's naive. "Doesn't she get it?" they say. "Doesn't she understand that she has a debilitating disease? She must be in denial."

I've seen denial and believe me, Jackie is not in denial. She is completely awake and aware and is one of the strongest women I've ever met. It isn't a physical strength; she certainly can't lift weights or run the marathon. Her strength is spiritual. It is absolute trust and faith that she's going to be okay no matter what happens. Her belief isn't dependent upon outside circumstances. It isn't dependent upon a doctor, a particular treatment. Her trust is solid because she believes in a higher power, in a universal energy, and in the love of the people around her. Certainly she is afraid. Of course she has days of worry, fear, and pain. The unknown is scary. But she turns to her faith in herself, her family, her friends, and in a higher power which she never even clearly defines. She trusted this power before she got cancer and she continues to trust it. It comes naturally to her. She has always had faith and unconditional trust. That's what trust is, unconditional faith.

❄ **Trust is an unconditional surrender to a knowing deep inside yourself that everything is all right, exactly as it is. The outcome is immaterial.**

Trust is a melting, a giving up of control, and the absolute knowledge that someone is running things. It's knowing that you'll come out all right in the end, no matter how it looks while it's moving along. It is an absolute belief that you will be okay and that you are not alone. This doesn't mean there won't be times when you question your faith or second-guess your beliefs or worry that no one is listening. It means you always come back to your faith.

Unconditional trust creates a kind of spiritual protection. Jackie trusts as I sit beside her that no matter what happens, I'll be there for her. And I will. She tells me how she appreciates me as a friend and how she appreciates her husband and trusts in his love. As she speaks, she teaches me that with trust comes a sense of safety. Her safety strengthens me and I take comfort in it. That's the way trust works. It's contagious.

My brother David, who died ten years ago, was the first close family member I lost. I was young at the time and my faith wasn't as strong, so after he died, I was angry at God. His death had really thrown me because I had prayed and prayed for him to live. I had done my best to maintain an unwavering faith in his survival. When he died, I said to myself, "See, it doesn't work. I prayed for a miracle and I didn't get it. Maybe there's no one up there listening. What if there just isn't anybody to trust? What if there isn't a God?" Have you ever felt this way? It's the most painful feeling I can remember.

Several years after my brother died, I lost my father. This too was difficult. I struggled with all the "whys" most people feel when something awful happens to someone they love. Then my sister Donna died. It was almost too much to bear.

As destiny would have it, on the day that I was the most depressed about my sister's death, my minister stopped by unexpectedly. Donna's youngest daughter, Lori, was with me that day, and she was in a tremendous struggle to accept what had happened to her mother. I was holding her and talking with her in an attempt to ease our pain. I remember saying to the minister, "The only positive thing I can find about my sister's death is that it has deflated some of my fears. The little things I was afraid of, the stuff I obsessed about, it all seems so petty now. I guess if it can't kill you, it really can't hurt you."

My minister looked me straight in the eye and with overflowing compassion he said, "Lucinda, even if it *can* kill you, it can't hurt you."

I'll never forget his words because in that moment, my heart melted and I felt my sister everywhere. There I stood with Lori in my arms, absolutely knowing that even though Donna's body had died, her soul lived on. I couldn't prove it, but then I didn't have to because I knew it for sure. In my heart. In my soul. In the body of my niece. It's not that I no longer feared death, it was still a big unknown. It's not that I no longer missed my sister. I still miss her so much, it hurts. It's just that as I felt her presence in that moment, and when I hold either of her daughters in my arms, I feel

Donna's love. I trust that love to uplift and sustain all of us. And I always will.

UPWARD DELEGATION

In my seminars, I often tell the participants to "let go and let God." I call this delegating upwards. My beliefs are Christian, and ever since I was a young child I have believed in God, even though the strength and conviction of my faith have gone through various stages and changes. In my lifetime I've lost my brother, my father, and my sister. Without my faith, I don't know how I ever would have trusted life or allowed myself to love other human beings for fear of losing them, too.

�֎ **Giving your problems to God is a powerful way to let go. When it works for you, and it will, you'll be able to use it whenever you are at a loss about what to do.**

What a sense of relief to delegate upwards and know that someone else is handling things! To illustrate this point, I'd like to share the following letter with you.

Dear Lucinda,

I still believe that God put me "onto" you guys and I believe with everything in me that your program is helping and will continue to help thousands of people.

I need to take a moment to tell you the rest of the story. How many times have you had mail delivered on Christmas Day on a Sunday? I live in a fairly large town, not small town USA where everyone knows the postmaster. This Christmas I was at my brother-in-law's house having Christmas dinner and the phone rang. Dave Miller was calling for me. I'm thinking to myself who is Dave Miller?

To make a long story short...it was a guy in the postal department who saw a package addressed to me. I have no idea what he was doing working on Christmas morning but he decided to deliver the package to me in person. The package being delivered to me that Christmas day was from my very best friend. When I opened it tears welled up in my eyes. In the package was a framed plaque inscribed just for me that read:

Susan... Trust me... I have everything under control.

—JESUS

Maybe it won't hit you like it did me but it only confirmed for me that God was looking out for me when your program came to me. I am not a religious fanatic in any way but you can bet who my "safe person" is these days. A combination of trusting God and applying what I've learned will see me through my moments of anxiety.

Susan

Faith is absolute belief that something will happen or that someone will be there for you. The tricky part: it isn't always exactly what you thought would happen or exactly who you thought would be there. Most of the time, when things aren't going the way I want them to, I can step back and say, "It looks like it's going all wrong, but that can't be true. I've given it to God, I've done the footwork required of me. If this is what's happening, it must be okay. It must hold some kind of merit I can't see yet."

I believe things happen for a reason. If the relationship ended, it was supposed to end because it'll be better for you in the long run. If your anxiety forced you to quit that job, there's probably a better one coming up. It reminds me of a saying I like very much and have found to be true over and over again. "When God closes a door, somewhere He opens a window." If you knew that for sure, you wouldn't be scared. The next time you are faced with a closed door, begin looking for the open window.

✤**Faith is believing in the process, no matter how it looks. It requires great patience and continued conviction that things will work out for the best.**

This is hard for people with anxiety. We want to do, to fix, to solve, to manifest, and we want to do it all now. Sometimes now isn't possible. Maybe your struggle today is the learning experience you'll use later to help others. Just because you can't see the window, doesn't mean it isn't there. Maybe by delegating upwards, it'll appear. Prayer is a wonderful way to practice having faith.

A simple prayer once changed my faith and my life and I decided that from that moment on, I would absolutely believe, unconditionally. When my daughter Brittany was three years old, David and I wanted to have another child. For reasons which were never clear, it wasn't easy for me to get pregnant. When I finally conceived two years later, we were all very excited. Three and a half months into the pregnancy, something didn't feel right. I began to spot and I miscarried. We were devastated. We were told that chances were slim that I would get pregnant again.

Several months passed and after a romantic weekend holiday with David, the miracle happened once again. We were overjoyed, but I was concerned. A week later, I noticed that I was spotting, just as I had done before the miscarriage. My heart sank. I wanted this baby so much. I began to cry. I couldn't go through it again. What if this were my last chance? What would I tell Brittany this time?

Spontaneously, I went into the living room, got down on

my knees and prayed. "Dear God," I began, "I really need to know that someone is listening and I really need this little soul in my life. If You will please allow it to come to me, I will never question my faith again. No matter what happens, I'll be a believer. I know it's wrong to say this but I've had so many losses in my life, I'm feeling alone. Please let this little soul come to me. I need it. I need You to show me that You're there." My words amazed me; I had no idea that I would say them, but they had poured out straight from my heart.

Immediately after the prayer I walked upstairs, I really didn't know why, and I opened my jewelry box. I took out a simple little golden cross on a chain and to this day I don't know where it came from. I put it around my neck and vowed, "I'm not taking off this cross until this baby is born." The next day the spotting stopped and didn't come back.

I had a wonderful pregnancy and I delivered a healthy, nine pound, ten ounce baby boy. I wanted to name him Oliver but Brittany started writing "Sammy" all over everything she could find. I looked up the name Samuele and found that it meant, "Asked of God." And so Samuele Garrison Bassett came into this world as a direct gift from God. From that moment on, I have had complete faith. I have been tested over and over again. Shortly after my announcing my faith, all kinds of challenges came into my life as if I were being tested and I kept saying, "It's okay, I know You're there." My prayers kept my faith intact and got me through my challenges.

THE GIFTS OF PRAYER

Besides allowing you a tangible way to communicate with your higher power, prayer can give you the opportunity to clarify what is bothering you, to put it into perspective, and to know that somebody else is sharing the burden. Prayer is God's gift to us and when we know how to use it most effectively, it can offer us great rewards.

A wise person once said to me, "When you pray, look for specific answers."

☙ **When you have a question, pray for an answer. Ask for a specific solution and then wait, watch and look.**

Your answer might come in the form of something you read in a book or something someone says or an event that unfolds. If you are watching for an answer, I sincerely believe you will get one. Prayer doesn't need to be a last resort. It can be a way of life. Find people who are on the same or a higher spiritual plane as you are. Read some good books, go to church or a synagogue or anyplace where you share spiritual beliefs with others so you can have some support and you can give some too. Use prayer to help strengthen your faith.

EPILOGUE

Is freedom anything else than the right to live as we wish? Nothing else.

—EPICTETUS

This is it. This is your life. What you choose to do from this moment on is up to you. No, it isn't easy and, yes, there are other people to consider, but ultimately, you are in charge of you. You decide what goes into your head and what comes out. You decide how you will react to the things and the people around you.

Freedom means choice. It means you can live the way you choose to live, do the things you choose to do. Freedom means you can be at peace with your choices and you can make the most of them. You can go to work, spend time with your kids, walk, run, and enjoy life. Whether it's cloudy, snowy, or 80 degrees outside, you're free. It's wonderful to get up in the morning feeling healthy and excited about life. It's wonderful to feel grateful to be alive and to look forward to a new day. Living isn't always easy or pleasant, but freedom isn't about things always being easy or pleasant. It's about making choices in keeping with what feels right to you. You can have the life you want and the freedom you deserve. You can have peace of mind by choosing the path to freedom.

Begin by remembering how special you are. Yes you are! You're smart, creative, intuitive, and compassionate. You're naturally sensitive to other people's needs and you're very loving. You have so much to give and so many different ways to express yourself. The world is an open book waiting for you to write the story.

You know that happiness isn't about money or things. It's about loving and being loved. It's about feeling content and fulfilled. It's about feeling useful and appreciated. We don't have to chase after happiness; it comes naturally when we feel comfortable with ourselves and who we are. Since we get up each day with the ability to decide to be happy, go ahead, make your day! And while you're at it, make someone else's. You know how to do it. You know how to change the way you think, talk, and react. Smile more. Pray more. Laugh more. Play more.

I am so grateful that I have conquered my fears and anxieties. I want the same thing for you so that you can experience life to its fullest. When I focus on the simple things, I remember my good fortune to have my life. I love to smell and experience the world; my eyes can't get enough of all the beauty. Now when I sit and hold my children I am in that moment, smelling their hair, holding their hands, watching their eyes sparkle as I tell them stories. No longer am I obsessing about some distant catastrophe. I'm there in the moment.

When I'm with my husband, I'm enjoying the intimacy and the affection, his warmth and touch, the scent of his skin. No longer am I analyzing a week-old problem and worrying about the day to come. I'm there in the moment.

When I'm by myself, driving in my car along a country

road, I'm immersed in the smells of the country, the colors in the sky, the music. No longer am I fearful of losing my mind, crashing the car, and running off the road. I am in the moment.

When I fly in a plane I sit back, relax, and gaze out the window at the beauty of the sky and the majestic view below. I chat with the people beside me no matter who they are or what they look like, because it's an opportunity to hear a new story. Everyone has something interesting to share. No longer do I sit and anticipate turbulence or a bad flight. I am in the moment.

I want to tell you about a recent day in my life that was very special. My mother was visiting and she, my little boy Sammy, and I went to a discount department store. We laughed and kidded with each other as we tried on clothes, wandered through housewares and the toy department, and we even snacked in the little snack area. It was such a treat to spend time with my mother and it was so much fun to watch Sammy with his grandma. We completely lost ourselves in the experience. Nothing special. Just a few hours in a discount department store. A few warm, relaxed, totally spontaneous and pleasant hours. Time passed. Precious moments.

Life is full of precious moments. Many of them come without effort. Most of them are free. Wallow in them. Let yourself be less anxious. Let yourself be happy. Allow yourself to be free.

My heart and prayers are with you on your path to peace.

❦ *Remember this—that very little is needed to make a happy life.*

—MARCUS AURELIUS

To my mother who taught me how to appreciate the simple
things in life.
Thank you… I love you.

❊ *Yes, there is a nirvana; it is in leading your sheep to a green pasture,
and in putting your child to sleep, and in writing the last line of
your poem.*

—KAHLIL GIBRAN

AUDIO PROGRAMS AVAILABLE BY LUCINDA BASSETT

ATTACKING ANXIETY

This powerful sixteen audio cassette program and workbook for anxiety and panic attacks is nationally acclaimed and is used by individuals and professionals at home and in clinical settings. A video of Lucinda in seminar is included. This self-help course will teach you how to:

- Overcome panic attacks
- Stop obsessive thinking
- Control fears
- Overcome your limitations
- Minimize or eliminate your need for medications
- Be more confident and more secure

Enjoy intimate conversations of others from all walks of life as they talk with Lucinda and share their stories of recovery. Listen to Lucinda and the medical experts and feel relieved as they disempower your fears and misconceptions. Thousands of people have been helped by these powerful tapes. Complete recovery is possible. Let these tapes show you how.

LIFE WITHOUT LIMITS!

How to Transform Worry and Fear into Positive Energy, Success, and Fulfillment

If you have recovered from your anxiety disorder and you're asking "now what?," this is the program for you. If you don't have anxiety disorder but you do worry, procrastinate, and let your fears hold you back, this program is for you.

Life Without Limits consists of eight audio cassettes, a journal of Potential, a 911 Feel Better Fast cassette, and a desk calendar. This compelling, motivating program will help you to:

- Understand the differences between men's and women's worries and frustrations
- Communicate better to get results
- Deal with anger more effectively
- Start dreaming again
- Define your goals and make them a reality
- Be a fabulous risk-taker
- Clarify your purpose in life

This wonderful life-changing program will help you stop worrying and start goal-setting. It will motivate you to move beyond your potential and live the life of your dreams.

For information and free literature about these and other audio cassette programs or to receive information regarding seminars in your area provided by:

The Midwest Center for Stress and Anxiety, Inc.
call: 1-800-944-9440
or write:
The Midwest Center for Stress and Anxiety, Inc.
106 N. Church St. Suite 200
Oak Harbor, OH 43449

For confidential phone support˙ with a trained staff call:
The Midwest Center Phone Support Line
1-900-407-4357

˙You must be eighteen years old to use this service; the cost of the call is $2.99 per minute.

INDEX